THE NEXT APPLE

HOW TO FIND STOCKS THAT COULD GO UP 1000%

TABLE OF CONTENTS

Intro - No Company Is Too Small To Succeed Or Too Big To Fail

"Change is the only constant." This is one of the most frequently used expressions in the financial world. And it's true – consider these early 2015 facts:

- Only 71 companies from the original 1955 Fortune 500 list remain today.
- Some of the biggest stock market winners of the new millennium were either near bankruptcy, small private companies or young IPOs 15 years ago. In other words, no one could predict how successful these companies would become, including the founders.
- None of the established big names from the 1990s turned out to be among the best performers in the 21st century.
- Some of the best performing stocks of the '80s and the '90s are bankrupt today or have been terrible investments in the new millennium.

In 2015, the world is more interconnected and changes faster than at any time in history. We live in an era where technology and society are evolving quicker than the ability of many organizations to adopt. Many simply cannot keep up with the pace of innovation, or after they reach certain size, they become too complacent and stop growing. Wall Street has never been a great forecaster, and the global, social, mobile world has only made forecasting and analyzing more difficult.

There are no sure things in the stock market. Nothing is promised or guaranteed to anyone. Yet every decade like clockwork, the stock market has delivered hundreds of stocks that go up 1000% or more. Even better, the best performing stocks have consistently shared similar characteristics.

The more the world changes, the more things stay the same. Patterns repeat in the financial markets. Only the names of the winning stocks change.

In the bull market run of the '90s, everyone won. Things turned upside-down after 2000. The first 10 years of the 21st century were not kind to the average investor. Some even ventured to call them the lost decade. The market survived several "once in a hundred years" crashes – in technology, housing and finance, yet at the end, most market averages recovered and made new all-time highs.

It took 13 years for the S & P 500 to substantially surpass its highs from the dot-com boom. If you invested a dollar in the S & P 500 in early 2000, you would have had a dollar by early 2013 - a dollar that would be worth a lot less at the time because of the diminishing impact of inflation on purchasing power. The S & P 500 basically delivered no returns for 13 years, but under the surface, there were huge winners among individual stocks. Fortunes were made and lost.

Ten-thousand dollars invested in Apple in 2003 is worth about $1.5 million in 2015. Despite two of the scariest recessions in financial history and enormous market volatility in the first 15 years of the millennium, the stock market provided the opportunity to invest in hundreds of stocks that went up 1000% or more.

The market is an opportunity machine. Some trends last only several quarters before they fade, while others continue for years and deliver fantastic returns. Sooner or later, though, every trend ends. This is not an opinion. It is a fact. Knowing when to sell is just as important as knowing what and when to buy.

This is not a book about the company Apple or its stock. This is a book about finding the next Apple or at least hundreds of "mini-Apples." The next Apple could and should change your life. The good news is that over the next 10 years – in *any* 10-year period – there will be multiple stocks that will advance a 1000% or more. The principles in this book will improve your odds of finding those stocks and, more importantly, riding them until it makes a difference in your returns.

The quality of our lives depends on the decisions we make every day. It's not a secret that the best return you will ever get is by investing in your own business. Not everyone has a brilliant idea and, more importantly, the means, the skills or the desire to build a great business. Let's get real – how many could actually create the next Facebook, Apple, Under Armour or Tesla? Warren Buffett says that he prefers to own part of a wonderful company than 100% of a so-so business. Everyone could invest in companies with great potential and participate in their growth. The stock market gives you that opportunity, but you also have to learn how to play the game. You have to learn how to speak its language.

If your goal is to achieve average market returns, just consistently put money into low-cost indexes and get it over with. If you are going to spend time, effort and money on learning how to invest, make sure it's worth it. The only reason to actively pick stocks is to achieve returns that will make a real dent in your universe.

When you are done with this book, you will know everything you need to know in order to find and profit from the next Apple, Starbucks and Tesla of the world. You will be a smarter and more knowledgeable investor.

Here is a brief sample of questions we answer in the book:

- Can you find the next Apple, Google or Tesla?
- Do what you love and success will follow is the most frequently given advice. Is "Invest in what you love/know" an equally bright idea?
- Does past performance impact future returns? The answer might surprise you.
- How to find the best performing stocks in any given year? It's a little counter-intuitive, but if you do what everyone else does, you cannot expect to achieve superior results.
- George Soros says that sometimes the market could predict its own future. Is the market always correct, and more importantly, how does that affect you as an investor?
- Timing is everything in investing. When is the absolute best time to buy, and which stocks should you buy?
- Some trends last only several quarters before they fade while others continue for years and deliver fantastic returns. Sooner or later, every trend ends. This is not an opinion. It is a fact. How do you make sure you keep your profits when a trend inevitably ends?

The only question that will remain is whether you will put that knowledge to work and create a better life for you and your closest people.

Ivaylo Ivanov (@ivanhoff)
Howard Lindzon (@howardlindzon)
March 2015

Chapter 1
Could Apple Be The Next Apple?

"It is the anticipation of future earnings that excites people, not the reality." - Darvas

Apple's Unique Growth Path

In 2003, Apple was a $10 billion company. In early 2015, Apple is a $750 billion corporation. That's a 75-fold difference.

It's difficult to remember how far Apple had fallen prior to Steve Jobs return. In the roaring '90s, when technology stocks were all the rage and just the extension ".com" guaranteed at least a billion-dollar valuation, Apple - the company that pioneered the personal computer - was a $3 billion dollar entity on the brink of bankruptcy. Its annual losses exceeded $1 billion, and its share of the PC market had shrunk to 4%. After rotating three CEOs, the board members had tried to sell the company, but found no buyers.

In 1997, Microsoft came to the rescue and invested $150 million in Apple. Two months after Apple's deal with Microsoft, Michael Dell told a tech industry conference that if he ran Apple, he'd "shut it down and give the money back to shareholders."

Steve Jobs returned as an interim CEO of Apple in September 1997. On a split-adjusted basis, Apple was trading at split-adjusted 80 cents per share at the time. It took Jobs and his team four years to release the first iPod. On the day of iPod's announcement, Apple was trading at $1.30 (adjusted for a 7 for 1 split). By 2004, many vocal skeptics and disbelievers still doubted Apple's comeback. Money Magazine ran a story titled "Why iPod Can't Save Apple." Apple hit new 3-year highs at $2 (split-adjusted), and it never looked back. By the end of 2005, it was trading above $10. Another 10 years later, it's the most valuable company in the world.

The Next Apple?

There are two major ways a stock could appreciate in long-term perspective: grow earnings and grow P/E, which is the price people are willing to pay for a company's earnings. The first one depends on a company's ability to execute and some other outside factors, such as competition and regulation. The second is almost entirely influenced by current market sentiment.

Could Apple – the stock – become the next Apple? Could one of the best performing stocks of the past decade become one of the best performing stocks of the next decade? If history is a good guide, it's very unlikely.

The biggest stock market winners of each decade are very different because of 3 main factors:

1. The law of big numbers
2. The law of high expectations
3. The law of innovation

The law of big numbers

Companies are worth a multiple of their earnings, and that multiple is often directly related to earnings growth rates. When you are growing rapidly, you are worth more. When people expect you to grow faster in the future, you are worth more to them today. Growing earnings and growing expectations at a high pace forever have one thing in common. You cannot do it.

Sooner or later, a fast growing company becomes a slow growing company. The market often anticipates that and starts to pay lower and lower multiples before there is evidence of actual slowdown. When this happens, the company's stock begins to decline.

Growing at 100% when your sales are $10 billion is a lot harder than growing at 100% when your top line is $20 million. It's simply impossible to compound at such a rate for more than several years unless you start from a very low base and you have serious protection against competition. Very few companies are able to achieve that. This is why most upside trends last only a few quarters.

It takes 2 to 3 years for a product to transform from an early adopters' toy to being massively popular. Every product has its natural life cycle.

The trick to sustain growth is to reinvest profits in order to find the next great product or to acquire it.

Apple managed to sustain its trend for so long because it was able to come up with a new catalyst every 2 to 3 years and to basically create new product categories. It redefined retail, music, computing, communication, entertainment, etc.

Apple's catalysts in the 21st century so far include the following:

1. iTunes
2. Retail Stores
4. The iPod
5. The iMac
6. The iPhone
7. The iPad
8. iPay
9. The iWatch

The law of high expectations

Why is it that the very same company sometimes gets valued at 25 times earnings and sometimes it gets valued at 100 times earnings? It all depends on people's expectations. Not so much expectations about earnings growth, but expectations about making money in that stock.

When a stock has been a really great performer for the past few years, it becomes a household name. It has extreme coverage from the press, social media and financial analysts. It's a lot more predictable, and it's much more difficult to surprise the market. When expectations are high and a company cannot keep surprising the market, there is very high probability of disappointing. Not if, but when this happens, look out.

The market could be generous and occasionally give the benefit of the doubt to companies with great growth potential, but it's not all-forgiving. If those companies don't start to meet the market's expectations in terms of earnings and sales growth, their stocks are likely to decline substantially. High expectations are even more difficult to sustain than high earnings growth.

There are very few sure things in life. Customer loyalty fades. Competitive advantages disappear. Pricing power goes away. Mind share dissipates. Earnings and sales growth slow down. In other words, circumstances change. But what we can always count on is that high expectations will eventually mean-revert. Most companies cannot accelerate their earnings growth fast enough to counter the decline in the market's expectations.

The law of innovation

Chris Dixon from a16z says that large, established companies typically go after good ideas that seem like good ideas to everyone else. Startups and younger, smaller companies go after good ideas that seem like bad ideas to almost everyone else.

Small, younger companies are hungrier for success. They have to go after crazy ideas that the big guys are not going to touch; therefore, they have a bigger chance of creating something completely new that's going to disrupt the status quo. Once they get some traction, they have a few options:

A) Sell to larger companies
B) Go all the way, become the next thing and, in the process, create great wealth for their shareholders.

When Google launched in 1998, it was very late to the search engine industry. At the time, search was dominated by large portals like Yahoo and AOL, which thought of search as a loss leader. Stickiness, or the ability to make people spend more time on your site, was considered the key to business success. Google had the opposite strategy - it was so incredibly good at showing search results that people would immediately leave the website.

Google tried to sell its technology for $1 million to one of the big portals. The CEO of the large portal tried it and said that Google's search engine worked too well and would make people leave its site too quickly. Google had amazing technology, which was considered a very contrarian business idea that none of the established leaders at the time wanted to try. Google had no clue how it would make money at the time, but it clearly figured it out.

The takeaway here is that big companies are working hard on good ideas that look like good ideas. They want to bet on a sure thing. When you're so big and have something to lose, you give priority to safety. You only need to get rich once, says Warren Buffett. If you realize this, you are going to do things very differently. You won't take on big risks. You won't risk something that is important to you for something that is not that essential. This is exactly how most big companies think.

A company that has already been successful for quite some time and grown into a giant is not likely to develop the next big revolutionary technology. Large corporations are interested in keeping the status quo and continuing to enjoy their market leader status. They often innovate through acquisitions, but those acquisitions rarely have big impact on market leaders' top and bottom lines. For example, when Google acquired YouTube for $1.6 billion in late 2006, it had already gone up 500% since its first trading day as a public company. By all measures, YouTube has been an amazing purchase, but since its acquisition, Google stock has gone up only 100% in the 9 years since.

Even if a big company is proactive and innovative, the resulting new products or services are rarely game changers for its earnings and sales growth. Apple did it with the iPhone, but Apple is an exception that was run by a visionary genius who wasn't afraid to make bold moves.

Coke and Pepsi didn't initially go after the energy drink market. Red Bull and Monster Beverage did, and they delivered incredible returns for their investors.

The Walkman had huge success, but its impact on Sony's bottom line was minimal. The iPod had huge impact for Apple when it was small company trying redefine the way we consume music.

The iWatch comes at a time when Apple is the biggest company in the world. Even if the iWatch turns into a billion-dollar business, it will represent less than 2% of Apple's projected 2015 revenue. Its overall impact will be too small to move the needle and accelerate Apple's growth.

The First Trillion-Dollar Company

Apple is likely to be the first company to ever reach a market cap of $1 trillion. In early 2015, it's almost there. Our goal should not be to find a stock that will go from $750 billion to 1 trillion, but to own the next stocks that will go from $1 billion to 50 billion, from $200 million to 20 billion or from $5 billion to 100 billion in market cap.

Apple, Google, Amazon and Baidu are well-known and established companies in 2015. But 10 to 15 years ago, they either were still private companies or fast-growing risky bets that not many were willing to take. The market didn't know how to properly price them. They had many skeptics and doubters. No one had any idea that they would reward their early shareholders so generously.

The next Apple and Google of the world are not likely to be the current Apple and Google. Ten years from now, they will still have an enormous impact on many people's everyday lives. They'll probably still be extremely profitable companies, but they will not go up 100 times, or even 10 times from their current levels.

The market is always the same because the market is always different. The names of the big winners change every 3 to 5 years – sometimes even more often – but they all go through similar paths. Studying their identical patterns could help us immensely in finding the next stocks that are likely to go up 200% in a year or 1000% in 5 years.

The vast majority of big long-term trends start with a breakout to new 52-week highs from a proper base. The underlying reasons behind this breakout could be very different.

Big Trends Start In Two Main Ways:

1) Price momentum leads and earnings are expected to catch up later. In this case, the market is forward-looking. Stocks could break out to new 52-week highs when earnings are either not existent yet or very low and the market is willing to pay crazy high P/E multiple for them. This is the story of the vast majority of momentum stocks. Apple, Google, Amazon, Baidu and hundreds of others have gone through the same path. The market gave them very generous premiums at the beginning of their price cycles, but those companies were able to meet and even exceed expectations later by delivering solid earnings growth for a prolonged period of a time. Thus, it's the anticipation of future earnings that often drives investing in growth stocks, not the reality.

2) Earnings growth leads, price momentum follows. Sometimes, the stock market is slow to react to a big change in earnings, especially when it doesn't involve a popular name in a sexy industry. Prices change when expectations change. Big long-term trends often start with a sudden explosion in earnings that alters the market's expectations. Many of the best long-term market performers belong to this group - Monster Beverage, The Middleby Corporation, Keurig Mountain Coffee, Home Depot, etc.

Great Growth Stories Are Never Cheap

Fast growing companies are rare, and they always trade at premium. Very few exciting growth stories emerge every year compared to the thousands of institutions that want to own them. There is a lot of money chasing a small number of great stocks. Of course, the market will sometimes overreact and push prices to levels that seem unjustified at the time. No one wants to miss the next Tesla, Google, Apple or Chipotle.

Investors with a bias against high P/E stocks miss some of the greatest stock market winners of all time.

The P/E ratio line of many long-term market winners ends up being downward slopping. P/E reflects the market's expectations for near-term growth. It's normal for a stock that grows earnings at 100% to trade at >100 times its P/E. It's also normal for market expectations to decline over time and, therefore, a P/E ratio to become a double-digit figure. If a company manages to grow its earnings faster than market expectations' decline, it will see its stock appreciate over time. The truth, however, is that very few companies are able to achieve high earnings growth for more than a few quarters. This is why most trends last only a few quarters. You could still make a lot of money riding those trends, but a real long-term stock winner is made by its earnings.

Consider the following growth stories:

Apple

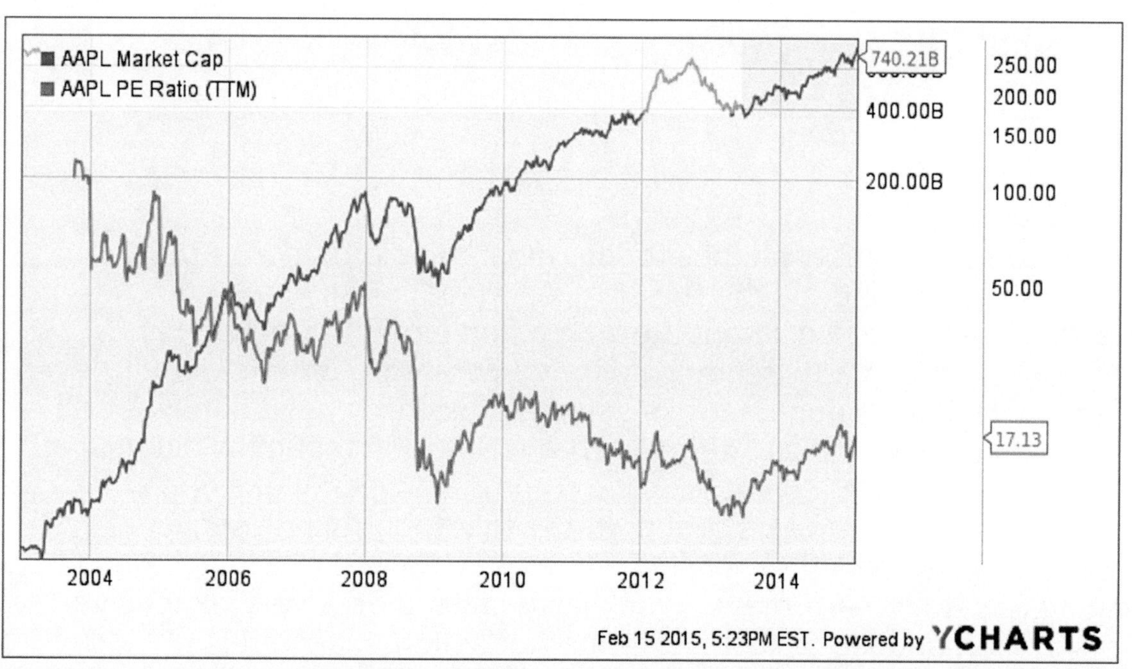

Long-term trends need to climb a wall of worry. Every trend could use a healthy portion of skeptics and disbelievers as they are a sign that there is someone left to buy. The story of the company Apple has remained the same for the past 12 years – it makes great products that people love and desire to have. The story of the stock Apple has changed dramatically.

Apple used to grow its earnings at a 200% rate in 2004, and the market was glad to pay 100 times P/E for its stock. As Apple grew bigger and bigger, investors grew more and more skeptical about Apple's ability to sustain its growth rate. Apple managed to outgrow people's skepticism by sustaining impressive growth numbers for a long period of time.

Between the end of 2004 and 2014, Apple's market cap increased 31 times. Its earnings growth was even more impressive – 126 times. Earnings growth was offset by an 80% decline in the price/earnings multiple that the market was willing to pay.

Apple, Inc.	2014	2004	Difference
EPS	$6.45	$0.05	126.5X
Revenue	183Bn	8.3Bn	22X
Market Cap	700Bn	22.5Bn	31X

Blackberry

When it comes to smart phones today, most people think of Apple, Google, Samsung and maybe the Chinese Xiaomi. Ten years ago, the kings of mobile were Nokia and Research and Motion (Blackberry). In 2003, Blackberries had already conquered corporate America, and they were just starting to appeal to households. Research in Motion was still an undiscovered $1 billion company that was losing money while having $300M in annual sales. Its stock cleared new 52-week highs and went from $5 to 150 in five years. Then, in the following four years, it declined 95%. It looked expensive all the way up and cheap for a good portion of its downward move. Blackberry started as a very expensive stock, but it managed to justify the market's high expectations.

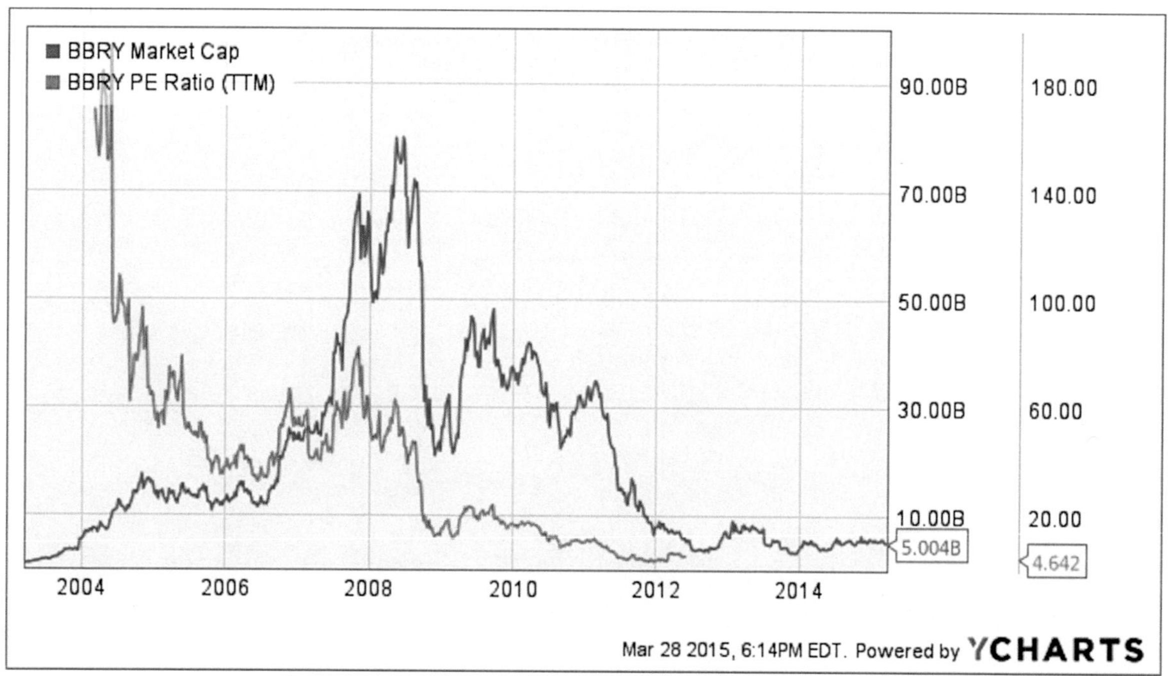

Google

When it IPO-ed in 2004, Google was a $40 billion dollar company with a P/E of 130 and earnings per share of $2. Fast forward 11 years, and Google is a $390 billion dollar company that makes $20 per share annually and has a P/E of 28. Its earnings are up about 10 times. Its stock is also up about 10 times for the same period. The difference is in the P/E, which basically measures the market's expectations. In 2004, Google was a young company that was consistently posting over 100% quarterly earnings growth; therefore, it was absolutely justified to trade at a high P/E multiple. High growth is rare, and financial markets reward it generously. As Google became a giant and its growth slowed down, though, the market's expectations declined correspondingly. Analysts expect Google earnings to grow 16% in 2015.

Baidu

Speaking of search engines, the biggest one in China – Baidu – has returned its investors even more money than Google. BIDU IPO-ed in 2005 at $27 per share, which is 2.70 on a split-adjusted basis (it had a 10:1 split in 2010). It was considered the hottest IPO of the year. Baidu gained 350% on its first trading day, finishing at $112.5 (12.25 split-adjusted).

Over the past decade, BIDU never looked cheap. It traded at high P/E multiples all the way from split-adjusted $2.70 to 220. There's an important lesson here. Don't be afraid to pay up for high-growth stocks with great potential. In many cases, they are expensive for a reason. Over time, earnings could more than catch up with people's expectations and justify high valuations.

This is exactly what happened with Baidu. In the quarter before its IPO, it earned $8 million. In its last quarter for 2014, Baidu earned $565 million.

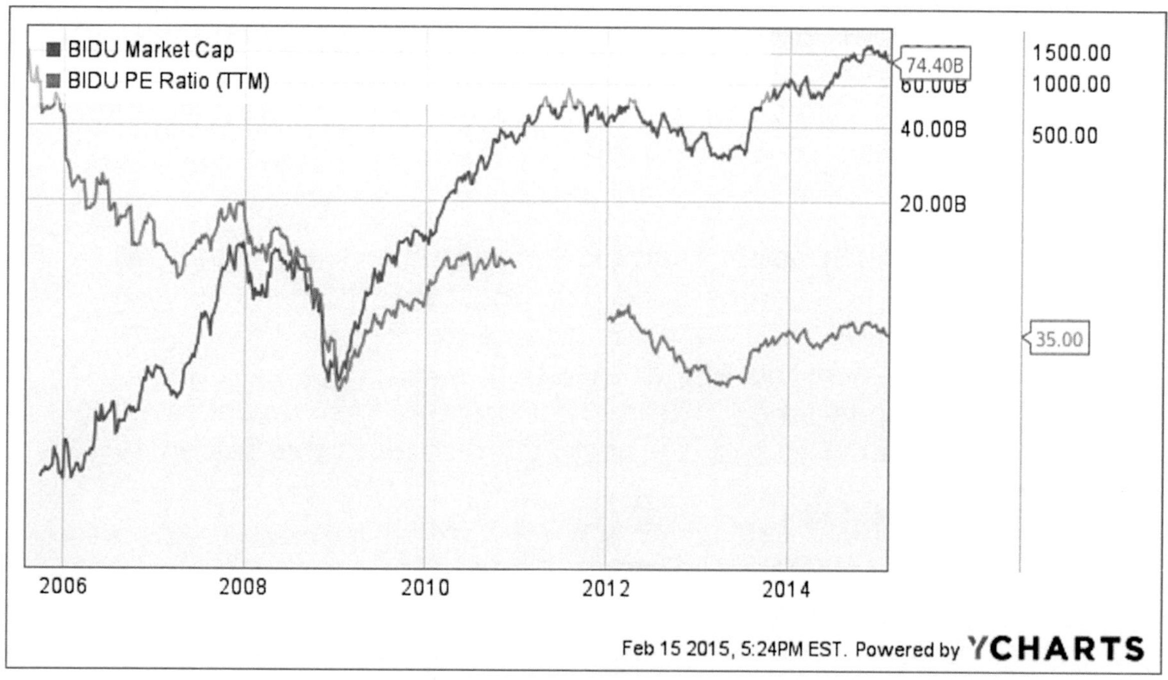

To paraphrase Benjamin Graham, the market is a voting machine in short-term perspective and a weighing machine in a long-term perspective. At some point, valuation matters, but only if earnings don't catch up, you plan to hold forever and you don't have an exit strategy. If price gets you in a trade or investment, price should take you out. If you don't know why you bought, you won't know when to sell.

Big Earnings Explosions Create Big Trends

Financial markets strive to be forward-looking, but not when it comes to underfollowed small cap stocks in obscure industries. Such stocks remain under the radar of most investors until they report huge acceleration in earnings growth. When a company that used to grow at 5 to 10% suddenly reports a 300% increase in earnings and a 100% increase in sales, it will grab the attention of many investors. It also will likely gap 10 to 50% to new multi-year highs. The good news is that this is often the beginning of a new powerful trend, not the end. Monster Energy (MNST) is a good representative of this category.

Such high-growth, under-followed stock is likely to go through 3 main stages:

1) Earnings growth leads price growth. There is sudden major acceleration in earnings growth that starts a process of re-pricing. Since the stock in question is still underfollowed, the market is likely to react slowly and under-discount this new potentially

disruptive trend. Most investors are still cautious with the new name. They either don't trust the sustainability of the story yet or haven't heard about it. A quarter with big expansion in earnings is like a cockroach. There is never only one.

2) After a few much better than expected quarters and major price appreciation, it becomes a momentum stock. Price starts to appreciate faster than earnings grow – the P/E multiple of the stock expands. At this stage, the stock and its story are widely known and understood. The market projects the current levels of growth into infinity, and it proactively discounts the best-case scenario.

3) There are two scenarios in stage three:

   A) P/E multiple drops: Price growth decelerates to the level of earnings growth, and both start to go hand and hand.
   B) P/E multiple declines: Price growth drops below the level of earnings growth, which means that there is a major correction – this is typical for most momentum stocks.

Growing Under the Radar

Some of the best long-term performers in the market are under the radar, boring businesses that grow 10 to 20% a year, pay regular dividends and have the power to easily pass raising costs to customers. The stocks of such companies rarely trade too cheaply to attract the attention of value investors. Since they belong to a boring industry that cannot grab the attention of the media and fascinate investors about their potential future, they also rarely become momentum stocks. They are not going to follow the typical pattern of a hot momentum name – go up 200 to 800% in a couple years, only to quickly give back 50 to 90% of it. Their stocks are likely to rise much more gradually, but consistently. Their price appreciation will track their earnings growth, and sentiment will have much smaller impact.

Earnings growth comes from two major sources:

1) Attracting more customers to spend more money.

2) Pricing power – the ability to raise prices faster than the increase in your costs. As Warren Buffett says, "If you have to light candles every time you raise prices by 10%, you are in the wrong business."

Costco, Middleby Corporation and O'Reilly Automotive are good examples that fit the above-mentioned description.

Costco has managed to grow its annual earnings by 10 to 20% for most of the period 1995 to 2015. Its stock went up 2000% in a 20-year period. Further, $1000 invested in the 1982 Costco IPO is worth about $170,000 in 2015. Not too bad for a boring retailer.

Middleby Corporation has a similar story, but with a twist. During the Gold Rush, most gold seekers didn't make much money. Whatever they made, they spent. The great wealth was created by those who supplied the miners – with food, clothes, tools and entertainment. The same business model continues to work flawlessly to this day. Middleby sells restaurant equipment. Most restaurants could only dream of Middleby's returns. From 1993 to early 2015, Middleby stock went from split-adjusted 50 cents per share to $107, a 214-fold increase. Restaurants as a group have not been a bad long-term investment either. According to Worden, the group is up 1800% since 1989, which is 3 times the S & P 500 performance.

And then there's O'Reilly Automotive. Could there be anything more trivial than selling auto parts? It's boring, but a very lucrative business. O'Reilly Automotive has been able to grow its earnings by 20% annually for most of the past 22 years (1992 – 2015). The result? An 8600% return for its investors.

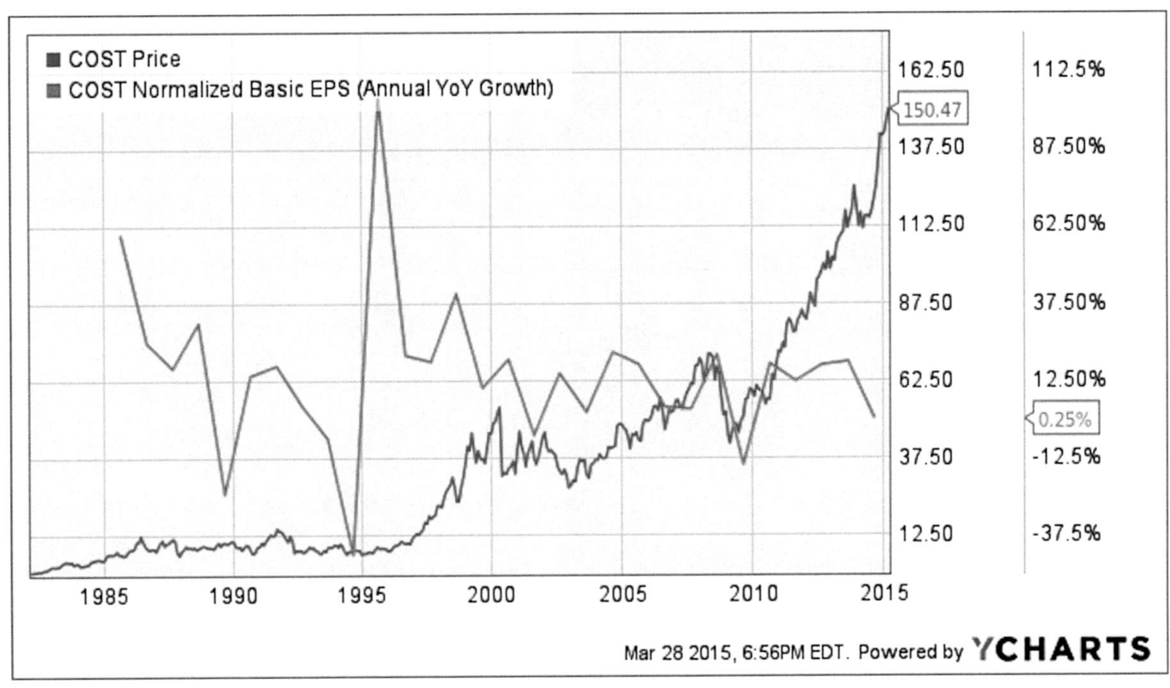

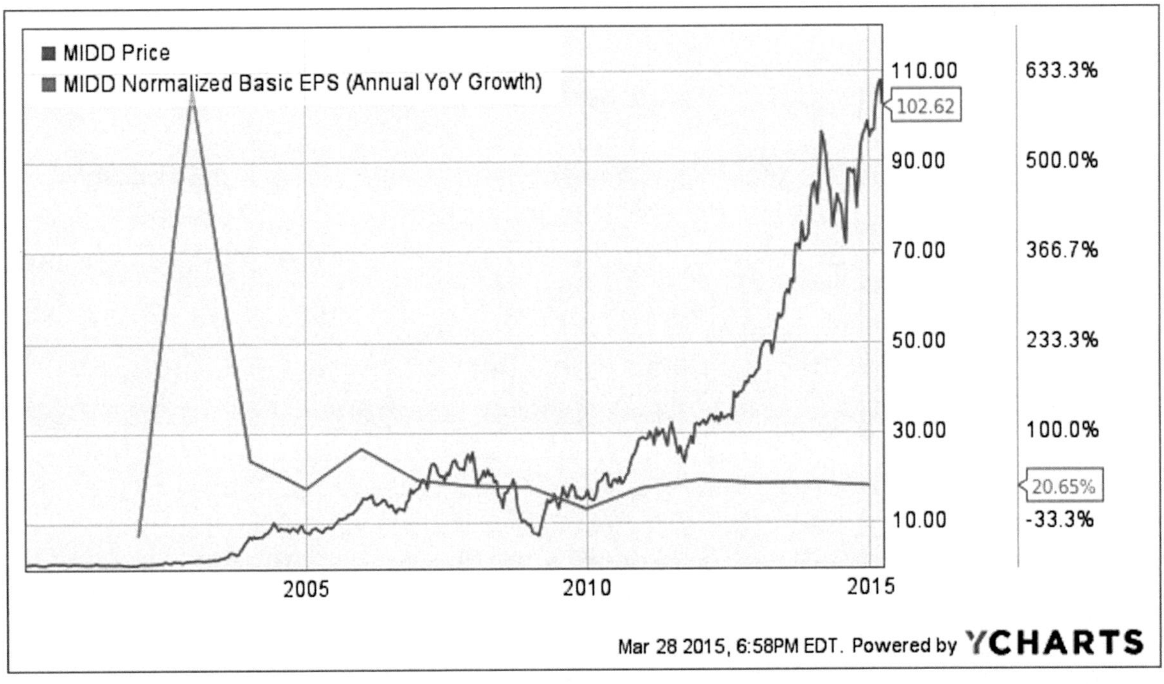

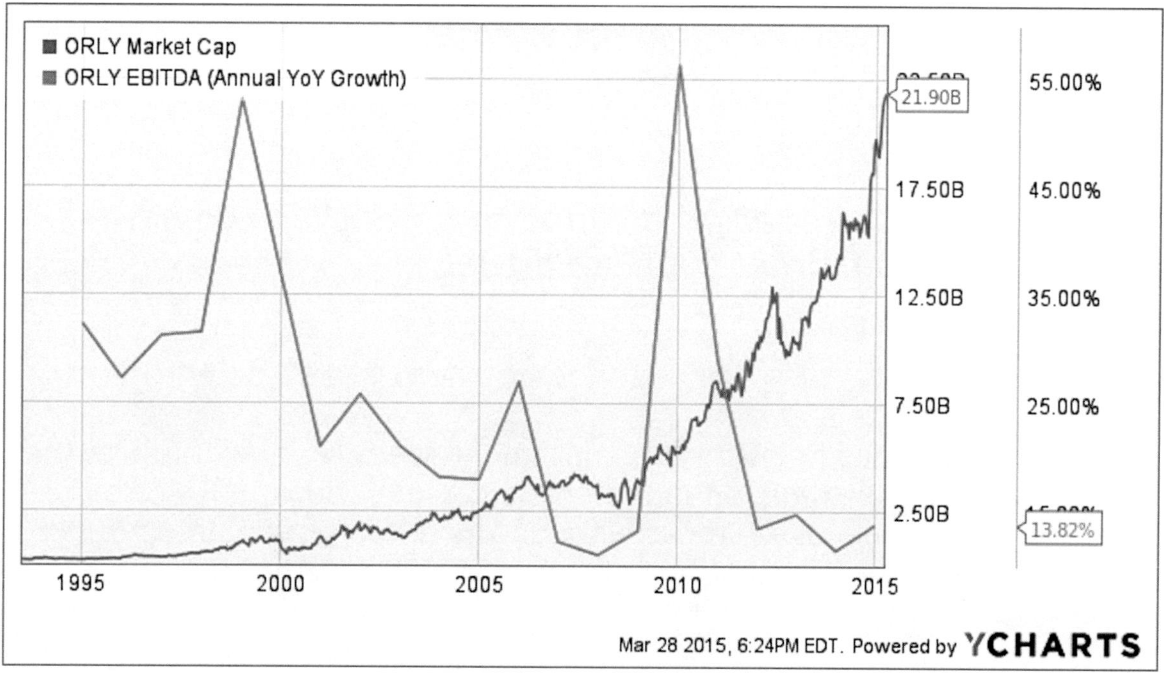

A Word To the Wise

Every study of past winners should be taken with a grain of salt because it has the inevitable element of survivorship bias. For each Amazon, Apple and Google, there are 50 others that didn't make it. Unfortunately, we can't study the future. Past data is all we have. Having a clue about the major traits that stocks should possess in order to have a chance to become big future winners is necessary but insufficient. Comprehending risk management is just as important, and we cover it later in the book.

Chapter 2
Perception Is The Reality

"The market is better at predicting the news than the news is at predicting the market." – Gerald Loeb

The Stock Market Is Forward-Looking, Most of the Time

The stock market has its own rules that might seem counter-intuitive to many. Stocks with incredible fundamentals could go down 50% or more during market corrections. Stocks without any earnings can go up 500% in a bull market. The allure of future earnings is what often drives investors' decision making, not the reality.

Some trends in the market are based on solid fundamentals. Others are based on wishful thinking. A good story about a tremendous future could substantially push up a stock price very quickly. It's not too unusual to see several hundred percent moves in a few quarters. The anticipation of growth rather than the growth itself could lead to great profits in growth stocks:

In 2012 - 2013, Yelp was considered to be at the perfect crossroad of three of the hottest trends at the time – mobile, social and local. Its shares tripled before it reported its first profitable quarter.

Tesla Motors went from $30 to 300 in 2013-2014 without a single profitable quarter. In fact, its founder and CEO Elon Musk warned the market that Tesla will reinvest its operating earnings and that it probably won't have any GAAP earnings before 2020. Early adopters loved its new car. In many people's eyes, Tesla was doing for the car industry what Apple has done for the computer and smartphone industries. The market gave Tesla the benefit of the doubt. It discounted a bright future. Of course, there's always a chance that its stock might turn out to be a flop, but that doesn't mean that you will have to give back most of your profits.

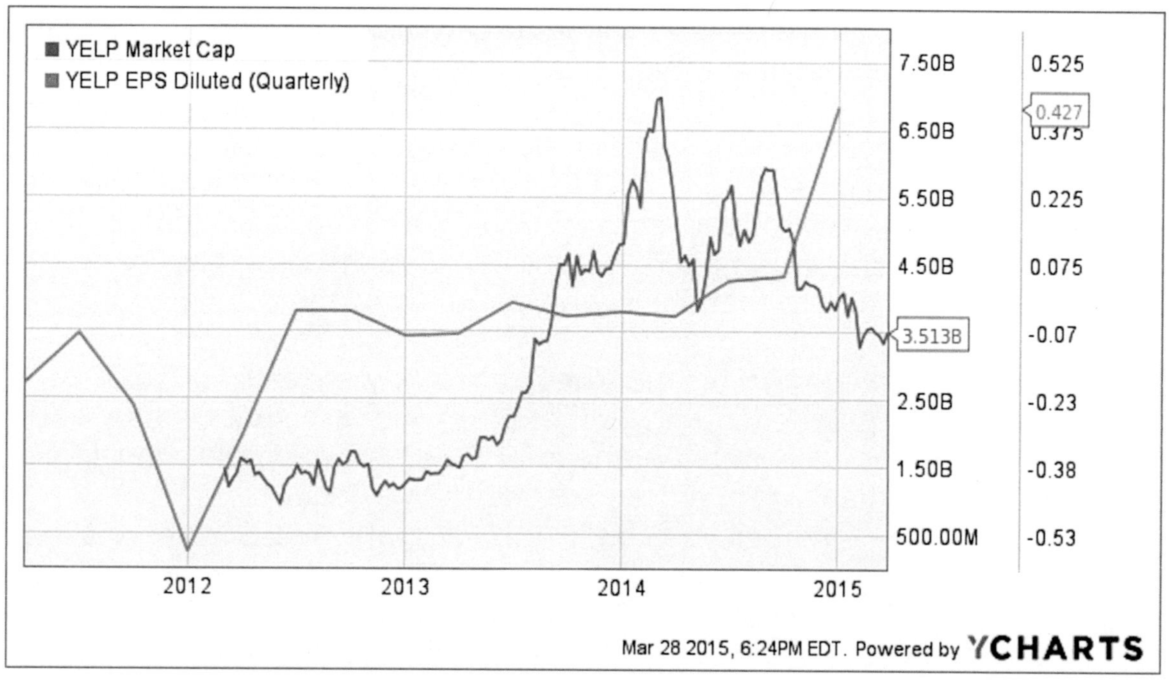

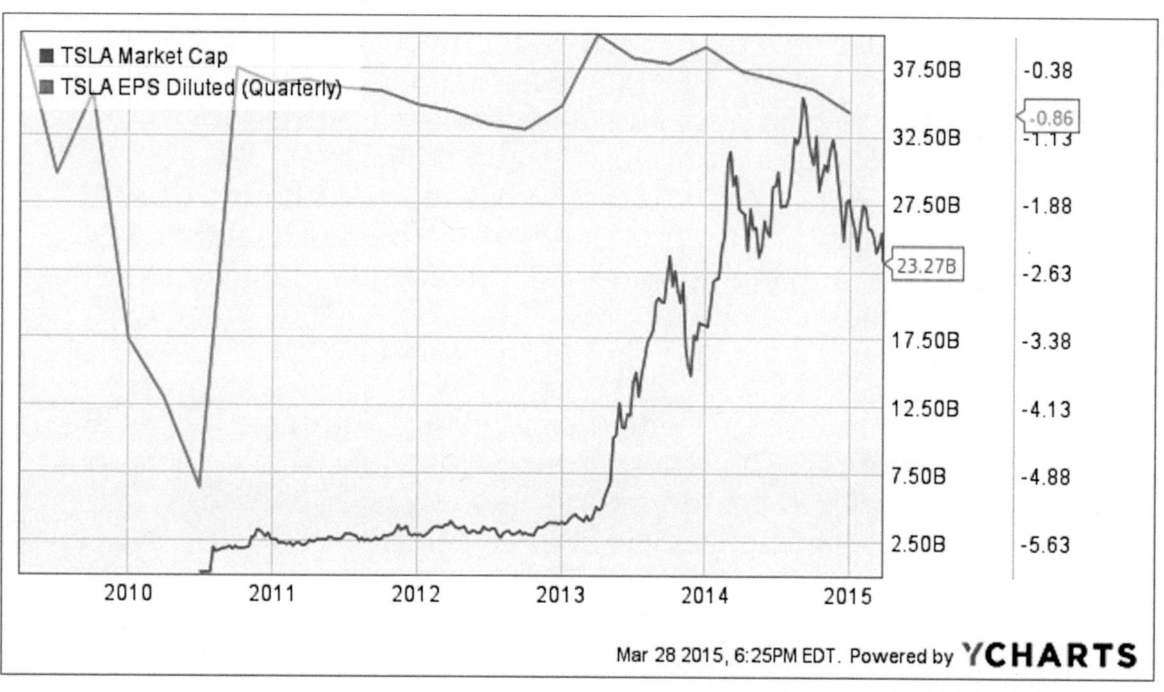

Blackberry quadrupled before reporting its first profitable quarter in 2003. At the time, its revolutionary products were taking over corporate America, and it was only a matter of time before households jumped on the train, too.

Anyone who waited for those companies to report their first profitable quarter before buying missed out on substantial gains. Anyone who waited for those stocks to become reasonably valued before buying missed out on their entire moves. Those three stocks are not exceptions. They represent the typical story of many momentum stocks.

Just because a company is not making money today, it doesn't mean that it won't start tomorrow. You should always ask yourself what the reason is behind the lack of current profits. Is it a flawed business model that is not likely to be fixed, or is it because the company is heavily investing today to make a lot more money in the future?

Financial markets live in the future. They constantly strive to price events that haven't happened yet. Sometimes, they are spot on and discount what will actually happen ahead of time. For example, housing and home improvement store stocks started to break out to 52-week highs in late 2012 – long before economic data confirmed that there's a housing recovery in the U.S. The market correctly predicted what was going to happen. By the time it was clear that the market had been right all along, most of the upside move in homebuilders was over.

By pricing events that haven't happened yet, financial markets will occasionally discount events that will never happen. Markets are not always right. A stock could quintuple based solely on investors' speculations and expectations for future profits. For example, 3D printing stock DDD went from $10 to 100 between 2012 and 2013. At the time, the whole world was excited about the possibilities that 3D printing could bring to manufacturing. 3D Systems did not live up to the expectations. The market became tired of waiting for the company to start making real money, and it sold the stock off in 2014.

Short-term price moves are based on sentiment. Long-term moves are based on earning power. The story, or more precisely, the expectations about a company have to come true at some point. Otherwise, disillusioned market participants will start to sell. The market is not always a brilliant, forward-looking mechanism, but it's also not stupid or naïve, at least not when given enough time. In short-term perspective, it could be all of the above times 10 and create results that are both irrational and unpredictable.

Is the Market Always Right?

Just because the market is forward-looking, it doesn't mean it is always right.

George Soros likes to joke that the market has predicted seven of the past two recessions. And he's right. Financial markets will sometimes discount fundamentals that will never become a reality.

Prices reflect people's expectations about the future, mostly about the near-term future. To say that the market is always right means to assume that people's expectations about the future always come true. We all know that this is not the case. No one has a crystal ball. People are often wrong.

The market is not always anticipating the future:

1. There are times when it simply corrects previously incorrect views. The market might be discounting the future, but it's not naïve. It doesn't wait forever. It constantly seeks positive feedback – in short-term perspective from price, in longer-term perspective from fundamentals. When expectations are met and exceeded, a trend is likely to continue. If a company doesn't live up to the expectations, there is often a swift correction. Most stocks don't

manage to live up to market expectations. This is why market history is full of thousands of examples of stocks that run 200 to 300% in a year or two, then give back most of it. There are very few stocks that manage to keep up with market expectations in the long run.

2. The discounting of the future is not a science. Sometimes it could be very emotional and quite irrational. Markets tend to overreact – to both perceived risks and opportunities. There are times when the market just goes bonkers and sends prices to levels that cannot possibly be justified by any future outcome. There are times when the fear of missing out trumps the fear of losing. People start to chase, price momentum becomes its own catalyst and short-sellers are mercilessly squeezed, sending prices higher with unimaginable velocity.

   As Paul Tudor Jones likes to say on such occasion, "Fundamentals might be good for the first third or first 50 or 60 percent of a move, but the last third of a great bull market is typically a blow-off, whereas the mania runs wild and prices go parabolic."

   In other words, very few investors are prepared for the last third of a move in a trend, when emotions override all reason.

Why Trends Exist

We know that the stock market is often but not always forward-looking, but how does that help us as market participants?

Being forward-looking requires the anticipation of future events. Discounting the future is a process, not a short-term event. This makes the existence of trends possible. Trends create opportunities to make a lot while risking very little.

Stocks are just like products – just like there are different buyers in the different stages of a product cycle, there are different people buying at every stage of a typical growth stock's price cycle. There are innovators, early adopters, early majority, late majority and laggards. There are various market participants with different philosophies and reasons to buy:

A) Some buy early, long before the crowd, because they understand or speculate about the potential impact a company or an industry will have. Some buy when a company is still losing money, but it has great potential, a great story behind it.

B) Some buy when a company breaks out to a new 52-week high from a proper base. This could happen well before a company reports any earnings or an improvement in growth. There are market participants who don't care whether the company is making plush bears or space rockets. As long as its stock price is making new highs, they ride it.

C) Some buy when there's fear of missing out. Institutions have to put money to work, and they have to choose assets to allocate to. At any given time, there are only a few great growth stories in the market and thousands of institutions that want to own them. In this case, P/E ratios often don't matter. It is all about catching the next big thing. Trends persist because supply is limited – early buyers are not eager to sell, and there are plenty of new buyers that would like to participate. There's a scarcity of great growth stories, and Wall Street loves growth.

D) Some buy when the company reports its first profitable quarter.

E) Some buy when a company has had several quarters of high growth and has a group of analysts that follow it.

F) Some buy when a company reaches a certain size.

G) Some buy because they are forced to cover their early/wrong short position. Every trend needs doubters and skeptics. Otherwise, there wouldn't be anyone left to buy. The existence of large short interest has fueled not or one or two big trends.

H) Some buy when a certain market cap is reached – some large funds cannot participate in companies with market caps under $5 billion because they cannot accumulate a position that is big enough to make a difference in their returns. When a company gets from $1 to 5 billion and it continues to deliver solid growth numbers, it will find a whole new set of buyers

On some occasions, market participants are forced to buy or sell regardless of price, which exaggerates current trends and the impact of newly discovered catalysts:

1) Forced liquidation during market corrections: This occurs when investors sell not necessarily because they want to, but because

they have to due to margin calls and redemptions from scared clients.

2) There is forced selling, but there is also forced buying When speculators bet against a stock and it keeps rising higher, they are forced to cover their positions and, in the process, become fuel for even higher prices.

3) Inflows of cash to mutual funds that require portfolio managers to buy every month disregarding of price.

How Perceptions Impact Fundamentals

George Soros is known as the "man who broke the Bank of England" in the early 1990s, but his main contribution to the financial world is the theory of reflexivity, which claims the following:

- Prices aren't objective. They're based on people's biased perceptions of the future.
- Biased perceptions define people's buys and sells, so perceptions will influence prices.
- Prices impact perceptions and fundamentals, too.

Soros's reflexivity theory is also a common-sense explanation of why trends exist.

What happens when a stock doubles in a year?

1) The stock market is considered a feedback mechanism. When prices go up, people assume that their initial investment thesis is right and that their expectations are justified. They buy more and are joined by even more people wanting to participate in the trend. The fear of missing out is ruling the market's behavior.

2) Higher stock prices mean happy shareholders. Happy shareholders mean a lot of good faith and patience for management. CEOs can make a lot bolder moves, and they are given more time to be right.

We have all seen the incredible faith that Amazon's shareholders have in Jeff Bezos. Eighteen years after its IPO, Amazon still loses money on the occasional quarter because it invests heavily in new projects. Amazon has missed more Wall Street earnings expectations than any other major U.S. corporation, yet its stock keeps showing up on the all-time high list.

Management is an important part of a company's fundamentals. When investors trust and believe management, they're willing to give the underlying company a lot higher P/E multiple. In other words, investors tend to trust managers who make them money. Earning shareholder trust by delivering them early profits does three key things:

A) Provides a lot of room for innovation and experimenting.

B) Helps to manage market expectations.

C) Allows focus on long-term goals while the rest of the corporate world is focused on the next quarter's results.

Most companies think about what will change in the next 10 years and try to position their businesses according to their projections and expectations. The truth is that no one knows what the next 10 years will look like and what novelties they are going to bring. The globe is moving faster than ever. Product cycles are a lot shorter. So is our attention span. Innovation is travelling faster than the speed of sound. We change our minds and preferences very frequently. Billion-dollar companies are made and ruined within the scope of a decade. It seems that change is the only constant, but is it?

Amazon founder and CEO Jeff Bezos doesn't think so. He thinks about what will NOT change 10 years from now and builds Amazon's long-term strategy around those constants. Lower prices, great service, faster deliveries and greater product selection – these are cornerstones that aren't going to change no matter what. People are not likely to ask to pay more, receive their deliveries slower, have less to choose from and receive crappy customer service. This is how you create a sustainable competitive advantage.

3) A company with highly appreciated stock could use it as a currency to acquire competitors and the best human talent in its respective field, which could make it a lot stronger functionally and operationally. We see how Google, Facebook, Apple and Tesla are scooping many of the best engineers in the world. We see how Salesforce is incredibly active on the acquisition field. Better prepared and more motivated people, new and better products, fewer competitors – these are all factors that actually improve a company's fundamentals, and they all could be derived from higher stock prices. The improved fundamentals attract a completely new set of buyers, which props prices even higher.

A good story could capture the imagination and change expectations. The dream of future profits is what excites people, not the reality.

This is how momentum works. But the process doesn't last forever. People's expectations about the future don't always come true. The market constantly tries to discount events that have not yet happened. As a result, it will sometimes discount events that will never happen. The market is forward looking, but at the same time, it's constantly looking for feedback: in short-term perspective from price, in longer-term perspective from fundamentals.

Sometimes, expectations turn into a self-fulfilling prophecy and end up impacting fundamentals. More often than not, the discounted future is way too optimistic or pessimistic. It's human nature to over-discount identified risks and opportunities. As a result, most trends last only a few quarters, but knowledgeable investors know how to take advantage of them and protect profits when the inevitable pullbacks come.

Chapter 3
IPOs – Every Finish Line Is the Beginning of a New Race

"The risk comes from not knowing what you are doing." – Warren Buffett

I don't know if a house is a good long-term investment, but putting money to work in home improvement stores has been a boon. For example, $5000 invested in Home Depot on its IPO day in 1981 is worth $23 million in early 2015. How much did your house appreciate for the same period?

The journey of every stock starts with an initial public offering (IPO). IPOs represent the first time private owners sell part of their company to the public – pension funds, mutual funds, hedge funds and individual investors. Once a company becomes public, its shares can be traded on the secondary stock markets, where everyone can buy and sell them. Companies such as Apple, Google and Tesla Motors are public companies.

Private companies are owned by their founders, employees, angel investors and venture capitalists. Just before a company goes public, new shares are issued on the name of the company, which is a separate entity. Those shares are usually sold to the public on the IPO day. Most of the money from the IPO proceeds goes into the company's coffers. Insiders gain a liquid market and ability to sell after lockup expirations, which typically last from 6 to 12 months after the IPO.

Why do private companies choose to go public?

1) Raise money for expansion, operational costs and strategic acquisitions. This used to be the main reason to go public. Nowadays, there is plenty of money in private markets for high-growth businesses.

2) Proper timing. Companies don't go public when they have to, but when they *can*. When investment bankers are confident in the current ability of the market to absorb supply from an industry, companies use the window to go public at proper valuation.

3) Receive valuation they cannot get in private markets. Bull markets can be very generous. The depth of the public markets' liquidity is still unmatched.

4) Create liquid market and an exit opportunity for founders, private investors and early employees.

Some IPOs provide incredible wealth-building opportunities by letting you participate in the growth of various great businesses. Let's take a look at the most successful IPOs in the past 30 years. Most of them went up 1000% in less than 5 years after their public debuts.

The Road to a 1000% Return

Company	Symbol	IPO		Reached 1000% Return in	February 2015	
		Year	Valuation		Valuation	Return since IPO
Microsoft	MSFT	1986	500MM	1990	347B	69300%
Whole Foods	WFM	1992	104MM	1998	19.3B	18400%
Qualcomm	QCOM	1991	412MM	1997	109B	26360%
Staples	SPLS	1990	204MM	1995	107B	52350%
Express Scripts	EXRX	1992	92MM	1997	60B	65100%
IAC Interactive	IACI	1993	51MM	1997	5B	9700%
Starbucks	SBUX	1992	111MM	1995	66.8B	60000%
Yahoo	YHOO	1996	551MM	1998	40.6B	7270%
Cisco Systems	CSCO	1990	279MM	1992	139B	50000%
Amazon	AMZN	1997	441MM	1998	173B	39130%
eBay	EBAY	1998	1800MM	1999	67.6B	3660%
Tesla Motors	TSLA	2010	2130MM	2013	26B	1100%
Pacira Pharmac.	PCRX	2011	252MM	2014	4.25B	1600%
Solarcity	SCTY	2012	768MM	2014	5.13B	560%

The worst thing you could do is to look at the table below and assume that buying IPOs is a sure thing. Far from it. Many IPOs turn into disasters for public investors. Don't buy blindly on the IPO day, no matter how much you like the company.

When you invest in an IPO, you need to understand your place in the puzzle. There are so many willing suppliers of stocks – VCs who want to bring back some money after years of waiting, employees who are in a hurry to taste their newly acquired wealth, investment banks looking for a quick flip. Unless new public companies report much better than expected earnings or have a fascinating story behind them, they often experience deep pullbacks as lockup periods expire.

Investors Have to Adjust Their Expectations for IPOs

A quick walk through financial history could tell us a lot about the major changes in IPO markets over the past few decades of 2015:

In 1980, Nike debuted as a public company by raising $5 million. At that point, Nike was already the biggest sport shoe company in the U.S. with enviable records of growth and a solid balance sheet. Today, there are startups without a product or revenue stream that raise more money in private rounds.

Apple's IPO was in December 1980. It sold 4.6 million shares at $22, raising about $100 million. It generated more revenue than any company since Ford's IPO in 1956. It instantly created 300 millionaires. By the end of the day, the stock had increased in value by almost 32% to close at $29, leaving the company with a market value of $1.78 billion.

In 1986, Microsoft raised $63 million by offering 3.1 million shares at $21. It had 24.7 million outstanding shares; therefore, its initial market cap was about $500 million. Don't forget that, at the time, Microsoft was already a well-known and extremely profitable company with 11 years of growth behind it.

In the midst of the biggest known bubble in financial history in 1997, Amazon went public at a $440 million valuation.

Do you notice the amounts that those tech giants raised on their IPO days and their initial valuation? They are giants today; they were giants back then – or at least notable leaders in their respective industries. Today, private companies without any revenues raise more money in private markets.

Nike, Microsoft Amazon and similar companies went public relatively early in their growth cycles. As a result, public investors had the opportunity to participate in 95 to 99% of their overall price appreciation. Founders, early employees and VCs took all the risk. Most of the reward was left for grabbing – anyone could've bought those stocks on the secondary markets.

As the Federal Reserve prints more money and interest rates remain low, an increasing percentage of capital is flowing into risky asset classes like venture capital and "angel investing." This capital has chased up valuations in the pipeline preceding IPOs, making the IPOs feel more like the end of the journey, not the beginning.

Thus, investors must adjust their expectations and understand the new metrics in the context of the speed at which companies are being created, growing staff and revenue, and expanding globally. The leverage in the systems from technology and the people web is mesmerizing.

Private Market Are the New Public Markets, In A Way

In the 2000s, companies that went public were 6 years old. In 2015, they are, on average, 10 years old. Not only are companies remaining private longer, but they're expanding much faster domestically and internationally, which means that they go public as much more mature companies and at a lot higher valuations. Is this good or bad? From one side, we have more mature companies that are less likely to fail. From another, it also means that public shareholders get to hop on the train at a much later stage of the growth cycle. The result is that the appreciation that normally would have happened in the public market is happening in the private market.

Companies go public at much higher valuations in 2015 for several fundamental reasons:

1) They remained private longer because they have access to capital.
2) They raised more money while private.
3) Today it takes a lot less money and time to start, sustain and expand a business.

The cost of building and launching a website went from $5 million to $5000 in less than 20 years. Today, there's an internet-connected computer device in everyone's pocket, and we're using them, on average, more than 200 times a day. In 2015, the iPhone is more powerful than many desktop computers 5 years ago. Computers are everywhere. The markets for them are expanding while the cost of attacking those markets is going down. It's a lot cheaper to market a product/service globally, and this is reflected in the valuations of private companies.

It has never been cheaper to start and to sustain a business. You can rent on-demand technology and expertise instead of owning or hiring full time. You can produce on-demand instead of building inventories. You can sell through the Internet instead of setting up an expensive brick-and-mortar shop. If you're on the Internet, the whole world is your market. Social networks like Facebook and Twitter have changed the way we make purchasing decisions. Yet it has never been more expensive to become a publicly traded company. As a result, many new companies remain private longer, raise more money in private markets and become public at higher price tags. Going public as more mature entities means that there is less risk for the public investor. Therefore, the valuations are naturally higher.

It has become harder to get small companies to market. The venture capital industry is playing the role that the public market used to play for micro-cap IPOs. As a result, nearly all of the market value of public technology companies is accruing while they are still private.

The IPO market has changed tremendously over the past few decades. It used to be that companies went public because they needed cash to expand. In 2015, high-growth companies can raise all the money they need in private markets. Look at the data below, and tell me if you notice a trend:

Total VC money ever raised by select companies:

Microsoft: 1MM
Apple: 3.6MM
Intel: 2.5MM
Cisco Systems: 2.5MM
Google: 25MM
Webvan: 441MM
Facebook: 2,426MM
Uber: 4,000MM

Uber went from a $4 million company during its first money raise to a $40 billion company in four years. Uber is an extreme example, but you get the point.

There is plenty of money in private markets. Companies with exciting growth stories can raise all the money they need or want in private markets. When such highly desired companies finally file for an IPO, a limited number of their shares are allocated to select funds. Usually, on their first trading day, such stocks will open substantially above their IPO price. In other words, ordinary public investors like you and me will get the chance to buy such stocks a lot later in their growth stages at very high valuations.

I'm not saying that it has become impossible to make money in popular companies past their IPOs. LinkedIn and Facebook are good recent examples of the opposite. I am saying that gone are the days when a market leader will go public and deliver a 10,000% or even a 1000% return.

Take a look at Twitter's venture rounds and the price action after its IPO.

Twitter's Venture Rounds and Liquidity Events	Valuation (MM)
Series A (2007) - raised $3mm	17
Series B (2008) - raised $22mm	70
Series C (2009) - raised $100mm	1000
2010 - raised $200mm	3700
August 2010 - raised $800mm	8000
December 2011 - raised $300mm	8400
IPO in December 2013: raised 2.09Bn	16000
End of first trading day	24000

It's very early to judge Twitter, but given its current market cap, it would be extremely difficult to become the next Microsoft or Apple.

We might not see as many 10-baggers in the public market due to major changes in financing and tech infrastructure, but public markets will remain a solid source of liquid opportunities. A lot more value will be created pre-IPO, but public companies with solid growth potential will still enjoy substantial returns.

How to Cope with the Change in Public Markets

If the majority of wealth nowadays is created pre-IPO, is there still a way for public investors to benefit from new listings?

The big money is usually made at extremes that are out of most people's comfort zones. In our eyes, there are two major ways public investors can approach the challenge of ever-changing IPO markets:

1) Go after stocks from hated, ignored or boring industries when they clear new all-time highs from a proper base. In this case, perceptions are worse than reality. Low expectations and new highs create a powerful combination.

2) Go after stocks from the hottest industries at the time when they clear new all-time highs from a proper base.

Those two approaches are diametrically opposing, yet they also have something in common – the requirement for a new all-time high. Why is it so important to wait for a new market issue to build a base and then break out to new all-time highs? Because it's an indication that a company's shares are accumulated by institutions. When institutions buy, they intend to hold for years, so essentially, they're removing supply from the market.
Now, let's go over each of those approaches and explain why they could provide you with an edge.

Go where Few Are Willing To Go

In bull markets, most companies go public at very high valuations by default. There are two occasions when valuations might be much more reasonable:

A) When a company goes public during market correction or after a prolonged period of market decline.

Rackspace went public at the worst possible time in recent financial history – the summer of 2008, when most people did not want to touch stocks with a flagpole. The rule of thumb says to ignore companies that go public during financial crises because raising money in crappy markets is usually a sign of desperation. Rackspace was about roughly a $1 billion dollar company on its IPO day in late 2008. In early 2013, it reached $10 billion market cap, before it gave up half of it.

B) When a company belongs to an industry most are afraid of or it's not enticing enough for most people to care.

Vips Holdings was one of the only two Chinese companies to get listed in U.S. markets in 2012. There were so many frauds related to Chinese stocks in the previous several years that, at the time, most people didn't even consider owning anything Chinese. VIPS opened as a $200M company in March 2012. In February 2015, its market cap is close to $15 billion.

When Solarcity (SCTY) IPO-ed in later 2012, the solar sector was one of the most hated and ignored – for good reason. It was down 90% for the previous four years. Solarcity had to slash its IPO offering from $13-15 to $8. By February 2014, it was trading at $88.

Emerge Energy Services (EMES) sells sand to oil and gas drillers. No one really cared about sand during the raging bull market in 2013. People usually don't care about sand in any market, which means when a sand company goes public, expectations are very low. Low expectations usually mean low valuation. The only way for a boring business like selling sand to get investors' attention is if it starts to deliver substantial earnings and sales growth. This is exactly what happened with EMES. It turned out that fracking (extracting oil and gas through horizontal drilling) requires a lot of sand, and sand companies were making a killing at the time. EMES went from $17 to 140 in about a year. Then crude oil collapsed and took with it all energy-related stocks. The lesson? Small float, a few better than expected earnings reports and a hot industry in a bull market can go a long way.

Many of the best performing IPOs of the seven years leading up to 2015 had an element of surprise in them. They either came from sectors that everyone hated at the time or they went public when people hated equities in general. In both cases, nobody expected them to perform well, which probably means that their valuations weren't too elevated. There was one more very important ingredient they all shared – they spent a lot of time on the all-time high list.

RAX Rackspace Hosting Inc. NYSE
©StockCharts.com
31-Oct-2012
Open 63.03 High 64.06 Low 62.40 Close 63.69 Volume 1.2M Chg +0.60 (+0.95%)
RAX (Weekly) 63.69 (31 Oct)
63.69
70
55
50
45
40
35
30
25
20
15
10
5
Jul Oct 09 Apr Jul Oct 10 Apr Jul Oct 11 Apr Jul Oct 12 Apr Jul Oct
VIPS Vipshop Holdings Ltd. NYSE
©StockCharts.com
27-Mar-2015
Open 28.45 High 29.03 Low 27.50 Close 28.62 Volume 21.2M Chg +0.21 (+0.74%)
VIPS (Weekly) 28.62
28.62
Had 10 for 1 split in Nov 2014
It was a $6 stock when it broke out to
new all-time highs in August 2012
24.0
22.0
20.0
18.0
16.0
14.0
12.0
10.0
8.0
6.0
4.0
2.0
0.5
M A M J J A S O N D 13 F M A M J J A S O N D 14 F M A M J J A S O N D 15 F M

SCTY SolarCity Corp. Nasdaq GM
©StockCharts.com
27-Mar-2015
Open 49.71 High 51.86 Low 49.03 Close 50.17 Volume 8.2M Chg +0.28 (+0.56%)
SCTY (Weekly) 50.17
90
85
80
75
70
65
60
55
50.17
45
40
35
30
25
20
15
10
N D 13 F M A M J J A S O N D 14 F M A M J J A S O N D 15 F M

EMES Emerge Energy Services LP NYSE
©StockCharts.com
27-Mar-2015
Open 49.14 High 54.20 Low 49.14 Close 50.96 Volume 1.4M Chg +1.41 (+2.85%)
EMES (Weekly) 50.96
140
130
120
110
100
90
80
70
60
50.96
40
30
20
A M J J A S O N D 14 F M A M J J A S O N D 15 F M

Go After the Hottest Industries of the Day

Recent IPOs in a hot industry can move substantially very quickly: 50% in a month, 100% in a quarter, several hundred percent in a year. There are always exceptions, but those moves are rarely sustained for long.
Between 1999 and 2008, crude oil went from $12 to 147 per barrel. This gigantic appreciation resurrected the clean-tech industry. For a few short years, the solar industry was the king of the market. FSLR went from $30 to 300 in 2007 after it cleared new all-time highs from a small IPO base. Then it dropped all the way down to $11 by mid-2012.

3D printing stocks were on fire in 2012 and 2013. DDD went up from $10 to 100 in 2 years. Such profits inspire and capture the imagination of the crowd. Such quick price appreciation is accepted as validation that all the stories about the potential of 3D printing will become a reality, which leads to a huge spike in demand for 3D printing stocks. No worries. The Wall Street printing and marketing machine is always here to oblige. If you're a company in a currently hot industry, the odds are that someone will call you and pitch the opportunity to go public right here, right now. This is how many industry trends end – by over-satiating demand. A couple new 3D stocks debuted on public markets in early 2013 – XONE went from $25 to 80 in 6 months. By early 2015, it was trading around $15. VJET went from $20 to 79 in 5 weeks. By early 2015, it was trading around $9 per share. The lesson? Don't overstay your welcome in recent IPOs that belong to a hot industry. Most of them will turn out to be short-term fads and will end up trading significantly below their IPO prices.

The same process happened in biotech stocks in 2013 and 2014. There are several dozen stocks that went up between 50 and 500% in a very short period of time. The odds are that the majority of them will give back most of their profits. The same patterns repeat over and over again because the incentives and the psychology of the key decision-makers haven't changed.

The proper timing of an IPO makes all the difference in the world. A bull market can be very generous and forgive all sins of speculators. All news is good news in a bull market. All news is bad news in a bear market. In 2014, any biotech IPO was eagerly awaited and generously awarded. Calthera Biosciences (CALA) and Coherus Biosciences (CHRS) went from $10 to 30 in the first three months of their IPOs. Atara Biotherapeutics (ATRA) went from $10 to 40 in six months. Cellular Biomedicine (CBMG) went from $5 to 40 in nine months. These are just a few examples of the crazy momentum that developed in the biotech space.

Don't overstay your welcome.

If recent IPOs belong to a currently hot industry or a company that is very popular on its own, the odds are that they went public at extremely high valuations. A quick and powerful rally after the IPOs has made them even more expensive – expectations are so high that it's pretty much impossible to meet in short-term perspective. Plus, financial markets are quite myopic – they're forward-looking, but don't look too far into the future. Recent IPOs are very vulnerable to mean-reversion after their initial rally, for several reasons:

1) Supply increases due to secondary offerings, lockup expiration and new IPOs in the same industry. It's perfectly appropriate for many of the new stocks that go up substantially in a short period of time to issue secondary offerings and dilute current shareholders. Wall Street is a printing press and a marketing machine. It carefully gauges the health of the market and the current appetite for certain industries. At the end of the day, it offers what the market desires. Supply is unlimited.

2) Companies don't live up to the expectations and don't provide the anticipated earnings and sales growth.

3) Enthusiasm eventually fades. People wake up. The fear of losing takes over the fear of missing out. The fear of holding the bag trumps the performance chasing and greed.

The vast majority of IPOs will go through a boom and bust process in a short period of time; therefore, the majority of them should be treated as short-term trading vehicles. Some of them will turn out to be big long-term winners, but you will have plenty of time to participate in their trends. There's no reason to hurry and buy them on their first trading day.

The Perfect Trading Vehicle

Recent IPOs could be among the most lucrative trading vehicles in bull markets. If you would like to find stocks that have the potential to run 20 to 50% in a 1 to 4 weeks, keep a watch list of recent IPOs with tight bases.

If you constantly study the stocks that gain more than 30% in a month, you will find many recent IPOs among them. There's a reason behind it. They have a lot going for them in a bull market:

1) Institutional support.
2) Insiders are locked and cannot sell for 6 to 12 months after the IPO.
3) Float is small, so even a little uptick in demand is enough to send shares higher quickly.

If you want to understand why IPOs are among, if not the best short-term trading vehicles, you need to educate yourself on the concept of float and what it means for supply/demand dynamics.

Float is the actual number of shares that is available to the general public.

Float = Shares Outstanding - Restricted shares

The number of outstanding shares is voted by the board of directors of each company.

Restricted shares are owned by insiders: founders, management, employees, VCs.

Companies always sell a minority stake during their IPOs. You will notice that most newly public companies' float is only 10 to 20% of their total shares outstanding. The rest are restricted shares. They are owned by insiders who are not allowed to sell for the next 6 to 12 months. This restriction is not created by the SEC, but by the underwriting investment banks in order to create a favorable market for new issues.

Google floated less than 20 million shares for its IPO in 2004. The rest became available 6 months after the IPO. In 2015, Google has a float of 620 million shares – in other words, it takes a lot more buying and selling power to move this ship.

Microsoft's float was only 20 million shares in 1986. In 2015, it's 7.6 billion shares.

More recently, Twitter IPO-ed with 70 million shares out of 615 million shares outstanding.

Small float, a bull market and a good story are an explosive combination of catalysts. When thousands of institutions compete to own a small number of stocks, we could see gigantic moves in short periods of time.

I elaborate on how to trade recent IPOs in my book "The 5 Secrets To Highly Profitable Swing Trading.". Check it out if you're interested in short-term market speculation.

Chapter 4
Is Investing In What You Love and Know A Good Idea?

"Common sense is not so common." – Voltaire

"Not everything that can be counted counts and not everything that counts can be counted." – Albert Einstein

There are two basic ways to come up with great investment ideas:

1) Start with price. This approach will give you ideas in areas you don't necessarily understand, but you don't have to in order to make money – or at least you could quickly educate yourself. There's always a simple explanation behind every move. Sometimes it's worth it to just close your eyes and follow price. We elaborate on this approach in the next chapter of the book.

2) Start with something you love or you have noticed that other people are going crazy about, and then check if the market is agreeing. Seeing your stocks on the 52-week high list is the market's way of agreeing with consumers.

The second approach was at the cornerstone behind the incredible performance of one of the best performing mutual fund managers in U.S. financial history – Peter Lynch. Between 1977 and 1990, he compounded at a 29% annual return, achieving a total gain of 2700% for his investors. During the same time, the S & P 500 appreciated 200%.

Peter Lynch retired in the early '90s, but he still remains the mutual fund manager with the best track record. His "secret" – buy what you know.

The best investment ideas will find you

How could your passion for a product or a service make you a lot of money? Everyone has a passion for something. Everyone is an expert in a certain area. Some enjoy building rockets. Some love shopping. Some like eating out. How many have ever tried to really make money out of their passions? They say that if you love what you do, you will be tremendously successful. The big question is, could you be tremendously successful if you invest in what you love? Yes, you could.

Warren Buffett states it best:

> *"People are going to get out of bed and work productively around the world to meet the needs of their family. People are going to spend and there will always be some companies that will sell something that people would love to trade their money against."*

Everyone shops, eats, wears clothes. Our consumer habits could be an excellent source of incredible investment ideas.

Products and brands come and go out of fashion. Many consumer trends last only a few years, but they could deliver 1000% returns before they end.

Do not be afraid to invest in places where you and your friends love to eat. Every decade gives us restaurant chains that transform many investors' lives. Chipotle Mexican Grill went up 1500% in its first 9 years as a public company. Dominos Pizza went from $10 to 100 between 2010 and 2014. Buffalo Wild Wings is up 1600% since its IPO in late 2003.

Some trends just hit you in the head. In 2006, you could see Ugg boots on every street in America. The stock of their Australian maker, Deckers Outdoors, went up 1000% between 2006 and 2011.

People vote with their dollars every day. So does Wall Street. Fashion constantly changes and brings new names on the scene. At least a couple years before Michael Kors went public in December of 2011, every woman knew it was the latest hot brand to own. Its stock went from $25 to 100 in the two years following its IPO.

By 2010, yoga had fully seeped into popular consciousness. Many bought $100 pants from Lululemon, but how many decided to invest in its stock? Lululemon went from $3 to 80 between 2009 and 2012.

You likely noticed that you and your friends or your kids went crazy about energy drinks in 2003. If you happened to check the stocks of the products you were spending money on, you would notice that a small company named Monster Beverage (it was called Hansen Natural at the time) was emerging to new multi-year highs. That later translated into huge gains for early investors – $5,000 invested in Monster Beverage in 2003 is worth about $2.3 million in early 2015. Not too bad for a sugary drink with a lot of caffeine.

BWLD Buffalo Wild Wings Inc. Nasdaq GS
© StockCharts.com
27-Mar-2015
Open 191.22 High 193.78 Low 178.47 Close 182.33 Volume 8.3M Chg -8.79 (-4.60%)
BWLD (Monthly) 182.33
2004
2005
2006
2007
2008
2009
2010
2011
2012
2013
2014
2015

CMG Chipotle Mexican Grill Inc. NYSE
© StockCharts.com
27-Mar-2015
Open 664.97 High 692.43 Low 652.30 Close 662.72 Volume 6.7M Chg -2.25 (-0.34%)
CMG (Monthly) 662.72
2006
2007
2008
2009
2010
2011
2012
2013
2014
2015

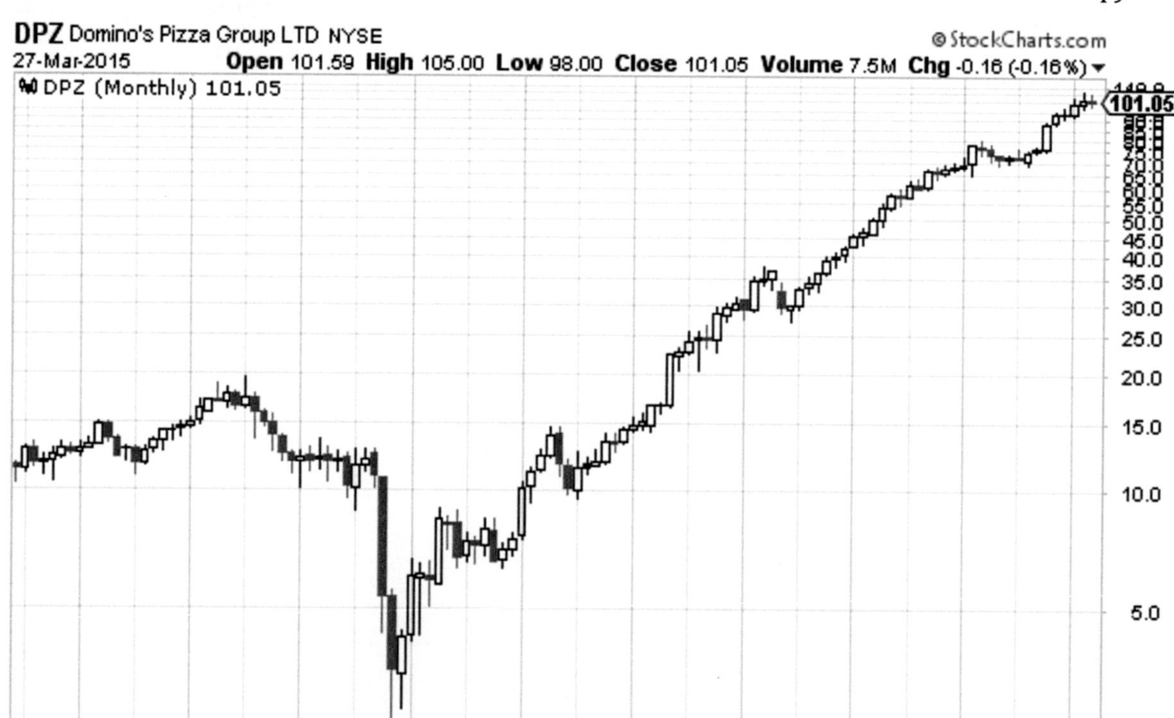
DPZ Domino's Pizza Group LTD NYSE
©StockCharts.com
27-Mar-2015
Open 101.59 High 105.00 Low 98.00 Close 101.05 Volume 7.5M Chg -0.16 (-0.16%)
DPZ (Monthly) 101.05
101.05
50.0
45.0
40.0
35.0
30.0
25.0
20.0
15.0
10.0
5.0
2006
2007
2008
2009
2010
2011
2012
2013
2014
2015

DECK Deckers Outdoor Corp. NYSE
©StockCharts.com
27-Mar-2015
Open 74.13 High 75.26 Low 69.93 Close 72.68 Volume 10.8M Chg -1.56 (-2.10%)
DECK (Monthly) 72.68
120
110
100
90
80
72.68
60
50
40
30
20
10
2005
2006
2007
2008
2009
2010
2011
2012
2013
2014
2015

LULU lululemon athletica Nasdaq GS
©StockCharts.com
27-Mar-2015
Open 68.59 High 68.99 Low 60.55 Close 64.32 Volume 50.3M Chg -4.12 (-6.02%)
LULU (Monthly) 64.32
64.32

KORS Michael Kors Holdings Ltd. NYSE
©StockCharts.com
27-Mar-2015
Open 67.46 High 68.93 Low 63.31 Close 66.97 Volume 55.4M Chg -0.44 (-0.65%)
KORS (Monthly) 66.97
66.97

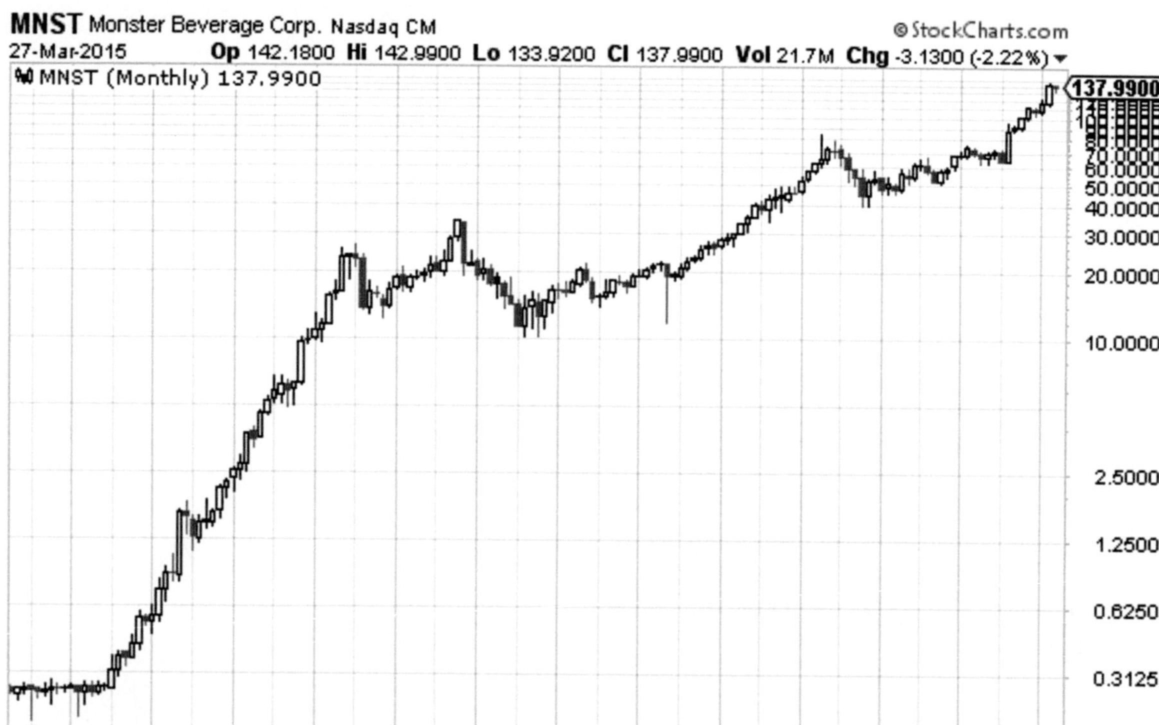
MNST Monster Beverage Corp. Nasdaq CM
©StockCharts.com
27-Mar-2015 Op 142.1800 Hi 142.9900 Lo 133.9200 Cl 137.9900 Vol 21.7M Chg -3.1300 (-2.22%)
MNST (Monthly) 137.9900
137.9900
70.0000
60.0000
50.0000
40.0000
30.0000
20.0000
10.0000
2.5000
1.2500
0.6250
0.3125
2003 2004 2005 2006 2007 2008 2009 2010 2011 2012 2013 2014 2015

NFLX Netflix, Inc. Nasdaq GS
©StockCharts.com
27-Mar-2015 Op 474.000 Hi 480.250 Lo 410.010 Cl 414.770 Vol 42.9M Chg -60.140 (-12.66%)
NFLX (Monthly) 414.770
414.770
200.000
175.000
150.000
125.000
100.000
75.000
50.000
25.000
6.250
3.125
2003 2004 2005 2006 2007 2008 2009 2010 2011 2012 2013 2014 2015

Here's Howard Lindzon on how he found and approached investing in two of the biggest trends of the past decade - Chipotle Mexican Grill and Apple.

Lindzon on Apple

My encounter with the iPod in 2005 is another good example of how I did some groundwork and experienced the product. I have never been comfortable with gadgets, but the iPod resonated with me the first time I picked one up. Then when I went to workout at the health club I would see a few people wearing those white iPod ear buds and I know in my heart that within a year or two, nine out of ten people will have those ear buds. I would not buy the stock because it was not even close to being at an all-time high; buying it then would have violated my boundaries.

But I did buy an iPod and I was using it, and it just so happened that an Apple store stood across the street from my office. I found myself in that store all the time and I noticed how busy it was and how much activity there was around the product. Eventually the stock started to moving up and the stronger it got, the more confident I became. I did not buy it at $12 a share, the approximate price at the time. I waited *until the stock tripled (still not all-time high) and by then it has risen to about $40 (pre-splits). I could not resist. I felt it in my bones.*

Sure enough, the white ear buds were all over the health club and the stock went up over 400% in the next two years. The iPod was a product I used and liked. It came from a place where I shop and was part of the lifestyle that I have adopted. The people around me also used it and liked it. All of those things gave me comfort in the catalyst for the stock. I could shut out the naysayers. I was actually emboldened by them, as they would be fuel for the fire when they finally purchased an Apple product. My investing standpoint was not all that different from my consumer stand point – I was part of the trend. I was not the first person to buy an iPod or Apple stock, but that didn't mean I couldn't make money.

Lindzon on Chipotle

Six or eight months after I had been eating at Chipotle once a week with my daughter, I heard that they were doing an IPO. I wrote about it, saying, "It doesn't matter what happens with this IPO. Whatever price it comes out at, it is a buy." I was confident after eating there all that time and seeing how they ran the restaurant, how four people could run an operation like that, and how simple the menu was. They also did the little things that made eating there a great experience. It was not like a usual fast-food restaurant, but the prices were pretty much the same.

What excited me most was they were in only a few South-western states, so they had a lot of opportunity in front of them. America had 300 million people. When you find a chain that is run the way Chipotle is, and then you see that it is in only a few states, you feel like you really have something. The really nice thing is that Chipotle is a cookie-cutter operation, meaning that they figured out how to run it, so it was just a matter of duplicating the formula. I believed it was a trend I could jump on. When your kid likes it and you like it too, it is an easy decision. You just know that you are going to make money with something like that. When you have that confidence, you can tune out a lot of the noise. When Chipotle came public, I bought it. The stock nearly tripled in eight months.

Howard elaborates on his social approach to investing in his first book "The WallStrip Edge".

The lesson? If you love a certain product or service and use it every day, if it makes your life better, the odds are that there are a lot more people that feel the same about it. We are much more alike than we think we are. We are wired to react similarly in the same situations and circumstances. Use that to your advantage. Think like an investor. Make the connection between a great product or service and the respective company's stock. Learn how to make money out of your own shopping habits, out of your friend's shopping habits.

If investing in what you love has been shown to be so simple and profitable, why are more people not doing it? Exactly. I've been asking myself the same question year after year as I see trend after trend. Most people simply don't think that way. Very few are making the connection between a product they love and the stock of the company that makes that product. Most people just invest in mutual funds and ETFs. They don't even think about individual companies.

You could own part of someone else's business. You might not have the say in what should happen, but you could participate in the growth of a hot brand as an investor. You could go to dinner at your favorite diner and make a lot of money while it's expanding. You could wear your favorite shoes and make a lot of money as their sales grow around the world and new outlets pop up everywhere. They say that the best investment you could make is in your own business, but in reality, you often have a much bigger chance of succeeding by investing in an already profitable, growing business as a public shareholder. Yes, it is true that you are getting the worst possible paper a company could issue - a common stock – but it's also true that you could make a lot of money doing it.

Quantifying Social Trends

You could connect the dots between your own, your family's and your friends' consumer habits and investing opportunities, or you could use a more scientific approach. Big data has revolutionized decision-making in many industries, including investing.

Likefolio is a website that helps the discovery process of hot consumer trends by scanning social media. It reveals in real-time what brands, products and services are getting more or less popular, and it quantifies people's sentiment toward them. Its sentiment data combined with a proper price filter could be a powerful idea generation tool.
Andy Swan explains how Tesla Motors popped early on Likefolio's radar:

When a company's primary product starts getting mentioned 20, 50, 100 times as often as it did just a short time ago.... there might be something significant going on.

Such was the case with Tesla a few years back.

People talked about Tesla 140 times as much at the end of 2012 (almost all positive) as they did at the beginning of 2012. 140 times!

When you combine this social signal with a breakout to new 52-week highs from a long technical base, you get a powerful investment idea.

A Company and Its Stock Are Not the Same Thing

Let's assume that you love a certain product, and you use it every day. What do you do next? Do you just buy and hold for years and wait for business growth to materialize in stock appreciation? What if everyone else has already noticed the same trend and invested in it?

Investing is never about just buying a piece of a business. It's about understanding how catalysts will change people's perceptions over time. Catalysts are earnings and sales growth, valuation, price momentum, market sentiment, competition, new products or services, management, new regulations.

Just because a product is popular does not mean that its stock will make you rich. You might be too early or too late as an investor. It's not an exception to see price trends end before earnings and sales growth slow down. You could lose a lot of money, or gain very little, if you buy a great business at the wrong time. Proper timing of your purchase is not just essential. It's everything.

The same Lululemon that went from $3 to 80 between 2009 and 2012 had a 50% correction in 2013-2014. The same Michael Kors that went from $25 to 100 between 2012 and early 2014 had a 40% correction in the year after that. The same Netflix that went from $30 to 300 from 2009 to mid-2011 had an 80% decline in the 5 months after that. The lesson? The stocks of products and services that you continue to love and use could have substantial corrections. Investing in what you love is a double-edged sword.

The outcome of your investment depends on the price you pay for it and on the price other people are willing to pay for it in the future. When you buy a stock, you are not buying a piece of business; you're buying the current expectations about the future of this business. Sometimes, it pays to buy extremely low expectations – the value investor's approach. Other times, it pays to buy rising expectations – the momentum investor's approach.

There could be a huge disconnect between the stock market, which is forward-looking, and people's passions, which exist in the present. I find it useful to combine the "invest in what you know" approach with the 52-week high list to make sure that the social momentum has materialized in price momentum. Remember, we cannot make a cent before the market agrees with our investment thesis. The market's way of agreeing with us is by sending our stocks to new 52-week highs from a proper technical base.

Early Adopters, Domain Experience and Investing

The easiest – and often the most reliable – ways to see the future and catch trends are pretty straightforward:

1) Look at the 52-week high list. It's often a shortcut to the minds of smart investors. It could also be a reflection of people's ignorance and stupidity. It takes some practice to learn how to use it properly.

2) Follow the thoughts of people with domain experience - angel investors, early adopters, engineers, specialists, venture capitalists, opinion-leaders. You don't need to know any people with domain experience personally in order to benefit from their wisdom as an investor. The beauty of the Internet and social media is that anyone has access to everyone's brain for a marginal cost.

If you learn how do both, you are likely to catch quite a few of the biggest stock market winners.

The good news is that you don't have to be first to recognize a new trend. The trick is to jump when it matters – when price, liquidity and fear of missing out start to drive investor behavior. It's extremely useful to follow and listen to early adopters in situations where financials alone might cause you to dismiss a great company.

One of the smartest posts I have read was written by Chris Dixon in 2013 – "What the smartest people do on the weekend is what everyone else will do during the week in ten years." In the post, he writes this:

> *Business people vote with their dollars, and are mostly trying to create near-term financial returns. Engineers vote with their time, and are mostly trying to invent interesting new things. Hobbies are what the smartest people spend their time on when they aren't constrained by near-term financial goals.*

Talking to smart people that are considered experts in their respective fields could give you a profound insight into future trends, but how actionable is the information you receive from them?

We have to be careful how we consume information. Everything we do, everything we read and watch impacts our decision-making, consciously or subconsciously. Talking to people who are perceived as experts in their fields could be a double-edged sword.

In April 2012, Howard Lindzon wrote a blog post to explain how he was convinced by a bunch of smart people to sell his Netflix position just before it quadrupled. It's a good lesson for all aspiring investors:

> *I have no position in Netflix. I put one in December (on the Stocktwits stream) when the stock was in the 90's and went to hang with some very smart people who had me convinced the Disney Deal was going to kill them. I let outside opinions influence (people I trusted that were super smart) the price and catalysts that were the reason for my investment in the first place. Now the stock has doubled. The catalyst may or may not be fully priced in, but Netflix is dominating on engagement and eyeballs.*

In February 2015, Netflix is trading near $480 per share. This is a typical example of how knowing too much and trusting perceived experts could hurt you. There is a saying on Wall Street - if you don't know why you are in a stock, then you won't know when to exit - which means that, in most cases, you will exit at a random point that doesn't maximize the potential of your investment.

From another side, I know people who have been bullish on Tesla months before the electric carmaker started to appear in the mainstream press and before people started to rave about its stock. Here is a screenshot of an email conversation I had in September 2012 with Dustin Schneider, who was one of StockTwits' leading engineers at the time:

Dustin Schneider <dustin@stocktwits.com> 9/10/12

to me

I like TSLA for 2 main reasons:

1) Elon Musk.
2) Heavy R&D and in-house manufacturing.

It may not be a good stock but it's a good company doing serious engineering led by one of the best visionaries of our generation. That's my two cents weither you want it or not.

...

Ivanhoff <ivanhoff@stocktwits.com> 9/10/12

to Dustin

long-term, they seem to be the major player in the industry. market is always short-sighted and doesn't look beyond 6 to 12 months which is a good thing for smart, patient investors, but you also need people with capital power (funds) to agree with you and buy the stock in order to make money.

...

You did not have to buy Tesla in September of 2012 to make money. If you did, your capital was allocated to an asset that went nowhere for 6 months. You could have waited for it to report better than expected earnings and gap to new all-time highs near $40 in April 2013. You would have still enjoyed most of the move afterward. Tesla Motors reached an all-time high of $291 in September 2014.

There are two types of catalysts - passive and active

Passive catalysts are value and the opinion of smart people with domain experience. They don't tell you when to buy or sell, but how far a move could go once an active catalyst is presented. There is only one actionable catalyst that matters: liquidity. In other words – only price pays.

Listening to geeks – engineers, industry experts, marketing gurus, experienced angel investors and venture capitalists, insightful visionaries and futurists – is always smart. They see and talk about future big trends before anyone else. Blindly acting on their recommendations in the stock market is a whole different game, though. I always like to repeat to myself that it doesn't matter how smart you are or how incredibly ingenious your investment thesis sounds. Unless and until the market agrees with you, you won't make a cent. The beauty of the stock market is that you don't need to be first or original in order to make money.

People with domain experience can see trends long before anyone else. This could be a huge advantage if it's juxtaposed with price (the ability to read charts). If price is not added as an additional filter, then three things are possible:

1) Experts could enter very early and put money to work in a non-performing asset. It won't start making any money before the market starts to agree with you. It might take months. It might take years. It might not happen at all.

2) They could, alternatively, stay too long and see their gains disappear. If you were a big believer in the potential of 3D printing stocks in early 2012, you made a lot of money. 3D Systems went up 1000% between early 2012 and late 2013. If you decided to hold your 3D stocks longer in anticipation of even bigger profits, you would've seen a 70% drawdown in the next year.

3) They also might see threats where they don't matter and exit trends way too early because of their deep understanding of a particular industry. They could be in too early and out too early and miss out on most of the gains. Comparatively, guys who rely primarily on price could catch the meatiest part of a trend without knowing much about an industry or the catalysts.

Why Even Bother?

If noticing a popular product or service is not enough to buy the stocks behind them, why do we even bother? Why don't we just pay attention to the 52-week high list and choose our investments from there purely based on price action?

What is the purpose behind investing in something you understand?

1) You might notice a trend before Wall Street. You don't want to be too early because your capital might be stuck in a non-productive

asset that doesn't generate any return. You don't want to be too late, either, and put money to work after major media outlets start to feature your stocks of interest in their primetime slots or on their front pages.

2) If you understand the catalysts, you're less likely to be shaken out by normal price pullbacks. You also won't pay attention to scary headlines with the singular goal of attracting more page views.

3) You're a consumer by default – we all are. We shop. We dine. How hard it would be to learn to connect products and services you love with their stocks? This approach has a proven record of great success.

4) Then, there is the question about further shrinking the universe of stocks you could invest in. In any given year, there could be thousands of stocks showing up on the 52-week high list. You cannot possibly own all of them. One way to capture big potential winners is to focus on trends, where you also participate as a consumer. Understanding the story behind a move is one very smart way to filter and limit the universe of stocks you're interested in.

5) Understanding the catalysts behind a price move justifies using a bigger position size compared to situations where price is the only reason you get involved.

6) Investing in what you love is not a flawless approach. There is always a danger that your love for a product could turn you into a biased investor with clouded judgment. Never love anything that cannot love you back. The market doesn't love anyone. It doesn't care about your personal agenda. Understanding the catalyst behind a price move could be extremely useful, but it's never enough on its own. Price action, on the other hand, could be a beginning and an end to your market approach on its own.

Chapter 5
Does Past Performance Impact Future Returns?

"The obvious rarely happens, the unexpected constantly occurs." – Irish proverb

"Sometimes being a contrarian means staying with the trend." – Steven Spencer

We all feel more comfortable investing in businesses we understand, in products we can touch, services we can experience. The big question is, are we not missing some incredible opportunities by focusing only on what we understand and can explain?

It does not matter how smart you think you are or how innovative your investment idea is. Unless and until the market agrees with you, you will not make a cent. The market's way of agreeing with you is by sending your long ideas to the new 52-week high list and even the all-time high list.

Since price is the only thing that pays, doesn't it make sense to rely on price action only for our buy and sell decisions?

Past Performance Could Be A Powerful Stock Selection Tool

Past performance is not a guarantee for future returns. It is the most standard Wall Street disclosure. Nothing is guaranteed to anyone. No stock picking criterion is flawless and works all the time. And yet, every year like clockwork, the same patterns repeat over and over again.

The beauty of financial markets is that you don't have to be first in order to profit from a trend. No one knows which new all-time high is the beginning or an end of a journey. No one knows how far a trend could go or how long it could last. Monster Beverage hit new 52-week highs in July 2003 and it kept going higher. Three years after its breakout, it traded 9000% higher.

Past performance could be an incredible source of investing ideas. By past performance, we mean two things:

1) Momentum – stocks that outperformed in the past three to 12 months tend to continue to outperform in the next three to 12 months.

   The father of value investing, Benjamin Graham, says that when people are shopping for common stocks, they should choose them the way they buy groceries, not the way they buy perfume. It is true that perfumes go in and out of favor and could be significantly overpriced, but no trend lasts forever, not in the market or in real life. There are trends that continue for only three months; there are trends that continue for three years. Both could be a source of substantial profits for an investor with basic risk management skills. Popular and overvalued is very different from going down tomorrow. You could never truly know where in a trend you are buying. Stocks could go up 100% in six months and then keep going higher for a lot longer than most people could remain solvent.

2) New 52-week highs – all long-term stock market winners spend a considerable time on the 52-week high list, if not the all-time high list. It helps you to find great investment ideas, for which you know very little about, but you could easily educate yourself. You don't need to be an expert in a field in order to invest in it and, most importantly, make money.

Momentum Works

There is no free lunch. Howard Marks from Oaktree Capital Group says that great performance today often takes away from future performance. It is like spending borrowed money—you will have to pay it back in the future, which will decrease your spending power.

Mr. Marks is right. The stock market is often forward-looking. Sometimes, it will even go insane and price a future that seems completely unattainable at the moment. The market could discount the next 20 years' worth of potential earnings, inside 12 months. The stock market constantly overreacts. A stock could go up from 20 to 200 in a year without having a single profitable quarter and then go sideways for 10 years or decline as its company starts to actually earn money. The good news is that we can participate in a trend on the way up and not give back most of our profits when that trend inevitably ends.

The Next Big Thing Is Often The Last Big Thing

People ask too often what the next big thing is. Sometimes the next big thing is the last big thing. Some trends last a lot longer than anyone could expect, comprehend or imagine.

Strong stocks leave traces, so you could participate in part of their trends. Take, for example, Pharmacyclics (PCYC). It doubled in 2011, quadrupled in 2012, doubled again in 2013, and basically finished flat in 2014, only to double again in the first three months of 2015, when it was acquired. During that time, it set up multiple technical bases and it broke out to new all-time highs hundreds of times. You did not need a time machine or inside information or expert knowledge on biotech to notice this trend. Price momentum was all you needed to spot and participate in this monstrous trend.

We could train ourselves to recognize good risk/reward setups, but we never know in advance how far a stock could travel. In his book *One Up*

on Wall Street, Peter Lynch wrote something similar about his biggest gainers:

"Frankly, I've never been able to predict which stocks will go up tenfold, or which will go up fivefold. I try to stick with them as long as the story's intact, hoping to be pleasantly surprised. The success of a company isn't the surprise, but what the shares bring often is."

Prices Change When Expectations Change

In his deeply philosophical book *The Most Important Thing*, Howard Marks shares the three stages of a bull market:

1) A few forward-looking people begin to believe that things will get better.
2) Most investors realize improvement is taking place.
3) Everyone concludes that things will get better forever.

This is an excellent description of the sentiment stages of the majority of the big market winners.

The stock market is often forward-looking. A stock could move to a new 52-week high long before its move is confirmed by fundamentals.

When a stock has been trading between 10 and 12 for, let's say, six months and it suddenly starts to change hands above 12, it is usually a sign that something major has changed, either in the fundamentals of the underlying company or in the sentiment of investors. Someone is willing to pay a price that no one else paid for a long time. Prices don't move out of a long-term range unless investors' and speculators' expectations have changed.

What could be the reason for such a change? Does the reason really matter? Isn't the result more important than its cause? The reason behind the change in expectations is not always important. It might be justified for some and not for others. In fact, for most people, the reason is irrelevant. As my friend and seasoned trader Brian Shannon likes to remind me, "price is the only thing that pays."

Someone might know something that most don't. By following price, you could become his or her silent "partner" and profit from his or her insights, reflected in price action. That person's knowledge could be based on insider information or it could be based on experience. The only reason we perceive the same situation differently is because we have had different experiences under similar circumstances or no experience at all. Maybe someone who has lived and traded through enough market cycles sees something that the majority doesn't and starts to buy before fundamentals improve or news is released.

The stock market is forward-looking. Prices don't change when fundamentals change. Prices change when expectations change, and the latter could change for various irrational reasons. By the time expectations are confirmed or disconfirmed by facts, most of the move might be already over. This is how financial markets often work. They are forward-looking. They price a future that hasn't happened yet. As a result, they will sometimes price events that might never happen.

The beauty of the market is that your broker doesn't care if you made your money in a trend that was justified by actual improvement in earnings growth or in a trend that was based on sheer speculation. A stock could go up 100% in 6 months without the slightest change in fundamentals. Everyone could participate in part of this trend without knowing anything about this stock. The money made or lost in trends we understand and the money made or lost in trends we don't understand have an equal weight. Only price pays, indeed.

Sometimes, Being A Contrarian Means Staying With The Trend

They say that the biggest opportunities are often outside of most people's comfort zones. The juiciest market returns are where very few are willing to go. Momentum investing is the ultimate contrarian approach. How many investors would venture to buy a stock that is already up 50% in the past six months? Psychologically, it is a lot harder to buy in this situation than to sell, isn't it?

How ridiculous does it sound that stocks that went up 50% in the past six months are likely to outperform in the next six months? Stock picking cannot be that easy, right? There has to be some complicated formula that takes into account hundreds of different criteria in order to have a chance at outperforming the market. Sometimes the most effective methods are the simplest. Most people stay away from them exactly because they seem too simple to work. There is nothing magic about using past performance to select future winners. It is all about simple math.

What do stocks that go up 200% in a year have in common?

Let's forget about size for a moment. Small-cap, small-float stocks are more volatile and more likely to experience larger moves, to the upside and the downside. What else do the best-performing stocks of each year have in common? It is not that they started their moves from new 52-week highs. In fact, some of them started from 52-week lows – typical, after the end of a major correction.

Before every stock reaches 200% return in a year, it is up only 50% at some point in that year.

Not all stocks that are up 50% in the past six months will continue higher. In fact, some of them will prove to be terrible losers.

But how do we know in advance which stocks that are already up 50% will continue higher and which will inevitably reverse lower? There are ways to substantially improve the odds of catching stocks with high potential to go a lot higher (which we cover later in this chapter), but the truth to the matter is that anything could happen. We don't know the future. And we don't have to. Using proper risk management is often just as good as knowing the future.

We dive deeper into the ocean of risk management in Chapters 7 and 8, but here's a brief overview.

The purpose of risk management is, well, to manage risk:

- To make sure that we pick stocks that have the potential to appreciate substantially.
- To make sure that our inevitable mistakes are not going to hurt our returns too much.
- To make sure that we stay with our winning stocks long enough to make a difference in our returns.
- To make sure that our winners are significantly bigger than our losers.
- To make sure that our position sizing doesn't hurt our performance, our sleep, and our confidence.
- To be active in the market when it is worth being active. To do nothing when there is nothing to do.

Here's a hypothetical example of how proper risk management could help you:

Let's assume that you have $200,000 and you allocate $20,000 to 10 stocks that meet your criteria. Three of them keep going up and deliver

50% return, while you are wrong on the other seven, but you keep your losses to 6% on each of them. What would be the end result?

50% return on a $20,000 allocation is $10,000

6% loss on a $20,000 allocation is -$1,200

3 x 10,000 – 7 x 1200 = 30,000 – 8,400 = $21,600

The beauty of the stock market is that you don't have to be right very often in order to make a lot of money consistently. There are people who are right only 30% of the time and still make millions every year. It is not important whether you are right or wrong; it is more important how much money you make when you are right and how much money you lose when you are wrong. Sometimes you will make a lot of money by blindly following a breakout in a momentum stock. Sometimes you will lose. How much you lose and how much you make will depend on two factors: 1) the market and 2) you. It is not true that you decide how much you lose and the market decides how much you make. Nope. A stock could triple, but it is up to you when you sell: you could sell when it is up only 20%, having no clue what the future holds.

In our hypothetical case, you were right on only 30% of your picks, but you still managed to achieve a decent return on your capital. What is the flaw of this example? While we could keep our losers small on most occasions, we have much less control over the size of our winners. They could be 50% or 5%. Well, this is why we pick from the bucket with stocks that are already up 50% in the past six months.

Stocks that are up 50% in the past six months usually have something going for them. It could be people's stupidity, but more often than not there is a good fundamental reason: acceleration in earnings growth, a better-than-expected earnings report, industry momentum. We might not know the exact reason, but we know that someone has been accumulating them.

Stocks that are already up 50% in the past six months have the potential to be either huge winners in the next six months or big losers. When we add a layer of risk management, we make sure that our losers are manageable and that our winners will be worth it. You could rightfully claim that the same logic could be applied to any market method. It is true: proper risk management is that powerful.

We are not simply buying any stock that is up 50% in the past six months. We just keep an eye on them and engage only when there is a breakout to a new 52-week high (sometimes a new 50-day high) from a proper technical base.

The 52-week High List Could Be Your Biggest Friend Or Your Biggest Foe

Sometimes, the 52-week high list is a shortcut to the minds of some of the smartest people in the world—people who see trends before everyone else and discount them in advance. The rest of the time, the 52-week list often a reflection of people's greed, unreasonable expectations, and outright stupidity.

When a stock reaches a new 52-week high, it means that someone has just paid a price that no one has ever paid for an entire year. Does that make him or her smart or irresponsible? It depends on the context.

Amazon was considered insanely expensive when it hit a new all-time high of $110 in 2009. It remained "expensive" all the way up to $310 in 2013. Many believed that Apple was a cannot-lose stock when it hit a new all-time high of $700 in September 2012 ($100 when split adjusted). It remained a "bargain" all the way down to $400 in the summer of 2013 ($57 adjusted for 7 for 1 split). After 40% drawdown, it managed to recover to new all-time highs.

Which new 52-week or all-time high is the beginning and which is the end of a journey?

Warren Buffett likes to joke that a bull market is like sex—it feels best just before the end. Many gigantic trends have started with a new all-time high, but also many trends have finished when there wasn't a single cloud in the sky.

Don't forget the stock market is one big house of mirrors, where many follow few. Almost no one is doing any real homework. Everyone is throwing a thesis on the wall and hopes that it will stick. Everyone is faking it until someone makes it. No one knows the future. No one is right all the time. Not all 52-week highs will turn into big winners. Sometimes, you will buy a breakout to new highs that will have all the characteristics of past winners, and you will still lose money. It is part of the game. Accept it and move on. The next big mover is right around the corner.

All big stock market winners appear multiple times on the new 52-week high list, but not all stocks that appear on the new high list turn into big winners. When you "shop" from the 52-week high list, you are shopping from a list of potential winners. The question is, which ones are going to continue to outperform? Which new all-time high is going to turn into the next 200% or 1000% gainer? While we cannot know that with any degree of certainty, there are ways to improve the odds in our favor:

What Will Help You Improve The Odds Of Finding Winners?

Three main factors:

1) Perspective

   The 52-week high list is a raw data point, which could be enormously useful if you know how to read it properly. Context is much more important than the data. If a stock is up 800% in the past three years, perhaps the market has gone too much ahead of itself. If it is over-followed by analysts and over-owned by institutions, the risk of owning might be greater than the potential returns. Of course, we never know how far a trend could go and how long it could last, but a proper entry point could improve our odds.

2) Catalysts

   Price often moves before any change in fundamentals, and yet some catalysts improve the odds of finding a winner with significant upside potential. Some catalysts have the rare impact of turning sidelined spectators into buyers and forcing short-sellers to cover their bets.

   A) When a breakout from a proper base is accompanied by a report of accelerating earnings growth that is better than expected, the odds are that we have a stock that is likely to sustain its move and go higher over time.

   B) When a breakout is in a currently hot industry, the odds are that it will follow through and deliver gains far exceeding the risk taken.

3) Technical Patterns

   We don't know where in its trend we are buying a stock, but this does not mean that we have to chase. We always look for a base that could define our risk. Why is buying a breakout from a proper technical base important? Because the formation of a base means that there is someone accumulating the stock. People (Institutions) would not accumulate a stock if they didn't expect its price to go higher. Their expectations could be founded on pure speculation or on sophisticated and comprehensive market research. There's no guarantee that they will end up being right and that we are going to make money following their footsteps, reflected in stock charts. We don't need to be right every time in order to consistently make money. The existence of a proper technical base helps us to define where we are wrong and where we should exit.

The same patterns repeat over and over again. The only things that change are the names of the stocks behind them. We look for two major types of patterns:

A) Continuation – stocks with established uptrends that are breaking out to new 52-week highs (or at least new 50-day highs) from tight bases on a weekly time frame. See some annotated examples below.

B) The beginning of a new trend – stocks that break out to new 52-week highs from a multi-month-long base on at least three times their average daily volume. See some annotated examples at the end of the chapter.

What About The 52-week Low List?

Stay away from stocks making new 52-week lows in a bull market. They are usually there for a good reason. Yes, you will miss the beginning of some turnaround stories, but you will save yourself a lot of trouble and, in general, you will do your portfolio a huge favor. If a rising tide cannot lift a boat, the boat probably has some serious leaks. It is the same in the stock market: if a raging bull market cannot push a stock from its 52-week low, there is probably something inherently wrong with the business of the underlying company.

It is always tempting to buy a stock that has declined 50% from its 52-week high level, but it is rarely a good idea if the drop occurs in the midst of a bull market. Many tried to catch the bottom in coal stocks after they plunged 50% in 2011. Then they dropped another 50% in 2012 and another 50% by mid-2014, and yet another 70% by early

2015. When all was said and done (we don't know if it is over yet), the majority of coal stocks were trading 95% below their all-time highs from 2011. In the midst of one of the biggest bull markets in financial history, coal stocks simply obliterated the capital of everyone who tried to catch their bottom.

Don't be greedy about turnaround situations in bull markets. They say that we should buy low expectations, and the 52-week low list is the ultimate symbol of low market expectations. The thing is that a stock that looks cheap could get a lot cheaper before it recovers. Big price declines are usually followed by a long period of sideways action, during which most market participants lose interest. Believe it or not, some stocks go to zero, and those that usually do spend a lot of time on the 52-week low list before they file for bankruptcy. Even if they don't go to zero, it might take years to recover. During that time, you could allocate your capital to a lot more productive assets, save yourself countless headaches, and actually make money. As the saying about stocks in a downtrend goes, if they don't scare you out, they'll wear you out.

Buying 52-week lows during bear markets is a completely different matter. When the general market goes down 10–20%, even the stocks of the strongest companies could decline substantially. There are some incredible bargains on the 52-week low list during periods of forced liquidation. But how do you recognize the ones that are likely to bounce and recover to new highs and the ones that are struggling for a good reason? You don't have to. You could simply wait for them to hit new 52-week highs. In fact, the ones that hit this benchmark first as the general market tries to recover are likely to be the leaders of the next bull market—the stocks that you must own if you want to achieve outsized returns. We elaborate on this subject in Chapter 7.

Sources

There are numerous free or really cheap sources for the 52-week high list: finviz.com, chartmill.com, barchart.com, investors.com, wsj.com, nasdaq.com, etc. There will be times when the 52-week high list has hundreds and even thousands of names every day, and it will be hard to sift through all the opportunities. This is a good problem to have. It is a sign of an expanding risk appetite, but a real challenge nevertheless. If you would like to take a shortcut, consider signing up for Social Leverage 50, which features 50 stocks trading near multi-year highs and possessing great prospects to substantially outperform the market averages.

BITA Bitauto Holdings Ltd. NYSE
©StockCharts.com
27-Jun-2014
Open 45.50 High 47.50 Low 43.82 Close 46.26 Volume 3.4M Chg +0.46 (+1.00%)
BITA (Weekly) 46.26 (27 Jun)
6-week tight consolidation
little known stock
breakout works
initial stop if wrong
failed breakout
sloppy base, up 5 weeks in a row
have to use very large stop loss
if you take it
Jun Jul Aug Sep Oct Nov Dec 2014 Feb Mar Apr May Jun
YY YY Inc. Nasdaq GM
©StockCharts.com
27-Jun-2014
Open 70.99 High 76.47 Low 70.21 Close 74.65 Volume 5.3M Chg +3.53 (+4.96%)
YY (Weekly) 74.65 (27 Jun)
raise stop after each breakout
stop below the most recent consolidation
perfect breakout
multiple weeks of tight weekly closes
stop is below the weekly consolidation
J J A S O N D 13 F M A M J J A S O N D 14 F M A M J

EMES Emerge Energy Services LP NYSE
©StockCharts.com
27-Jun-2014 Open 93.57 High 98.76 Low 89.95 Close 96.49 Volume 2.8M Chg +3.57 (+3.85%)
EMES (Weekly) 96.49 (27 Jun)
you could increase position on each successful breakout
perfect breakouts
raising stops
Apr May Jun Jul Aug Sep Oct Nov Dec 2014 Feb Mar Apr May Jun
CSIQ Canadian Solar Inc. Nasdaq GM
©StockCharts.com
3-Feb-2014 Open 39.13 High 39.90 Low 35.25 Close 35.99 Volume 4.8M Chg -3.14 (-8.02%)
CSIQ (Weekly) 35.99 (3 Feb)
sloppy wide-rage bases
but breakouts work, because of
strong industry momentum
A M J J A S O N D 13 F M A M J J A S O N D 14 F

GGAL Grupo Financiero Galicia S.A. ADS Nasdaq CM
©StockCharts.com
27-Mar-2015
Open 25.69 High 25.78 Low 23.22 Close 23.50 Volume 2.6M Chg -2.19 (-8.52%)
GGAL (Weekly) 23.50
breakout from a perfect base
stop
23.50
J J A S O N D 14 F M A M J J A S O N D 15 F M
AMZN Amazon.com, Inc. Nasdaq GS
©StockCharts.com
12-Mar-2010
Open 128.30 High 134.20 Low 127.71 Close 131.82 Volume 30.7M Chg +2.91 (+2.26%)
AMZN (Weekly) 131.82 (12 Mar)
good breakout
aggressive stop
conservative stop
131.82
M J J A S O N D 09 F M A M J J A S O N D 10 F M

TSLA Tesla Motors Inc. Nasdaq GS
©StockCharts.com
5-Apr-2013 Open 42.36 High 46.68 Low 40.21 Close 41.37 Volume 30.2M Chg +3.48 (+9.18%)
TSLA (Weekly) 41.37 (5 Apr)
MA(10) 37.50
MA(40) 32.71
Volume 30,180,020
new all-time highs
huge volume
BIDU Baidu, Inc. Nasdaq GM
©StockCharts.com
22-Jun-2007 Open 14.40 High 15.82 Low 14.35 Close 15.65 Volume 139.7M Chg +1.34 (+9.37%)
BIDU (Weekly) 15.65 (22 Jun)
MA(10) 13.18
MA(40) 11.14
Volume 139,738,880
clears IPO highs

Chapter 6

How To Find The Best-performing Stocks In Any Given Year

"To make money, you must find something that nobody else knows, or do something that others won't do because they have rigid mind-sets." – Peter Lynch

There is a saying that in the stock market, the obvious rarely happens and the unexpected constantly occurs. Nothing else describes better the true nature of the market. It could sometimes be quite counter-intuitive.

The biggest opportunities are often disguised and exist in industries most people are not willing to touch.

In 2012, the conventional wisdom was to stay away from all Chinese stocks. Their economy was slowing down. Their stock market was a mess. Their earnings numbers were questionable. As a result, only two Chinese ADRs made their debut on U.S. exchanges that year: Vipshop Holdings (VIPS) and YY Inc. (YY). Both of them formed solid technical bases, broke out to new all-time highs, and never looked back.

Don't assume that you know everything. The market is frequently a lot wiser than you and discounts events and processes long before they become mainstream. What you don't know won't hurt you, but what you think you know when it isn't so will. Don't let your biases blind you. Pay attention to price action.

It happens over and over again and it will continue to happen, because this is how financial markets work.

I constantly watch the all-time high and the 52-week high lists to get a sense of emerging trends and gauge overall risk appetite. Both lists are extremely useful equity selection tools, and they have been home to all big stock market winners at some point in their history.

An all-time high is not an automatic buy signal for me. I have always considered the technical characteristics of the stock (is it just breaking out from a long base?) in order to minimize risk of involvement. I also pay attention to the catalyst behind the breakout and the growth prospects of the underlying company. All those requirements have proven to be good filters over time, but with the price of numerous unwanted side effects.

Here's how overthinking has robbed me from some great market opportunities:

February 2011 – tobacco stocks were clearing major multi-year highs on strong volume. I disregarded the signal, conceptualizing that smoking is dying and that tobacco companies will only see their revenues decline. Philip Morris (PM), Lorillard (LO), and Altria (MO) gained more than 50% in the next year.

June 2011 – I noticed that more and more utilities were showing up on the all-time high list. I knew that it was never a good sign when defensive stocks were on the all-time high list, but I'd never really considered owning them, because they were not real growth stocks. Many of those same utilities went on to significantly outperform during the carnage of 2011 summer as capital went to perceived safety.

September 2011 – a bunch of REITs and home improvement stores (Home Depot, Lowes) were breaking out to major multi-year highs. I ignored those moves, thinking that no one wanted to own those slow-moving, boring stocks; besides, I reasoned, there was no way those moves could be sustained, with housing prices still under pressure at the time. Many of them went up 30%+ over the next six months as Home Depot reported solid earnings growth and rents reached all-time highs all over the U.S. Even homebuilders like Lennar (LEN) started to emerge to new highs in early 2012.

April 2012 – airline stocks were showing up on the 52-week high list—I couldn't believe it! I quickly disregarded those moves as noise, recalling that airlines had historically been terrible investments. Two years later, all airline stocks had more than doubled.

In hindsight, everything seemed so clear, but in real time it is never so. The point is that we have no idea how far a stock might go after it breaks out to all-time highs from a solid base. It might go up 15% and then fizzle, or it might go up 50% or 200%. We don't know that in advance, and we have no control over it. Good risk/reward technical signals have to be taken. Focusing on price action alone helps to minimize underlying biases.

ALK Alaska Air Group, Inc. NYSE
©StockCharts.com
9-Nov-2012
Open 19.20 High 20.34 Low 19.16 Close 19.95 Volume 10.0M Chg +0.81 (+4.23%)
ALK (Weekly) 19.95 (9 Nov)
19.95

ALK Alaska Air Group, Inc. NYSE
©StockCharts.com
27-Mar-2015
Open 68.68 High 69.00 Low 62.77 Close 65.59 Volume 6.1M Chg -3.09 (-4.50%)
ALK (Weekly) 65.59
65.59

When you find yourself surprised to see certain stocks on the 52-week high list, there are two possibilities:

1. You don't know the whole story. The perception is worse than the reality. The market might be discounting something you don't know.

2. Whatever it is you think you know does not currently matter. The worst has already been discounted. Everyone who wanted to sell has already sold, and a whole new set of buyers is now stepping in, changing entirely the supply/demand dynamics and probably starting a new price cycle.

What hurts you is not what you don't know, but what you think you know that isn't so.

If you let this concept become a cornerstone of your market philosophy, it will become a lot easier to find and own stocks that are likely to deliver substantial returns. Why is this the case? Because in any given year, the best-performing stocks are the ones that surprise the most—the ones for which the expectations are very low and yet start to rise in price.

Expectations could be low for two basic reasons:

1. A stock is neglected. No one is paying attention to it. It is often trading under $10. It has a small float and market cap, and its daily volume is relatively low. Liquidity often follows price momentum, and price momentum follows change. Sudden change means opportunity.

2. The stock of interest and its industry are universally hated.

Some of the biggest mistakes in our investing lives are often mistakes by omission. The biggest regrets always come from positions we could have taken, but for subjective reasons and irrational biases we did not.

Don't assume that you know everything. The market is frequently a lot wiser than you and discounts events and processes long before they become mainstream. Don't let your biases blind you. Pay attention to price action.

The more you think you know, the more closed-minded you are, which poses a two-fold danger:

1. Overconfidence in your current positions will blind you to potential threats.

2. Overconfidence in your current positions will blind you to great market opportunities. If your approach tells you to buy a stock and you ignore it because of personal biases, then you should force yourself to buy it anyway. The odds are that a lot of other investors will feel the same way as you and are going to pass on that opportunity. As Jesse Livermore put it, "successful trading is always an emotional battle, not a battle of intelligence." If you want to make a lot of money in the stock market, you have to do something that most are not willing to do.

The best-performing stocks in any given year are the ones that surprise the most, which means that they are very likely to come from an industry almost no one expects.

In late 2011, housing-related stocks started to clear 52-week highs. No one believed in their moves, because of their horrid performance in the previous few years. They ended up being the hottest sector in 2012.

Solar stocks were left for dead between 2009 and 2012. Things took a 180-degree spin in early 2013, when many of them broke out to new 52-week highs. No one trusted these range expansions. In most people's minds, solar stocks were still garbage that should not be touched. By the end of the year, many of them more than tripled.

The surprise factor is the essence behind this approach. There are two ways a stock could shock the street:

1. Reports could be much better than expected earnings and guidance, giving a lift to the whole industry. The initial market reaction is what is important here; if the market does not care, we do not care, and we move on.
2. It comes from an industry no one expects to be performing well. The market is often a forward-looking mechanism that discounts six to 12 months in advance.

As Howard Marks likes to repeat, "the big winners come from the so-called high-risk categories, but the risks have more to do with the investors' perception than with the categories."

One of the most powerful combination of catalysts is a new 52-week high + high short interest + very negative sentiment—so negative that people don't even want to listen to you when you start talking about that industry. The only way to make big money in the market is by being right about something that the majority of people have gotten wrong.

The patterns repeat over and over again. The only things that change are the names involved. When everyone hated banks in 2010–2011 and no one wanted to touch them because they were all considered black boxes and the market always pays lower valuation for higher uncertainty, a small bank based in San Diego was breaking out to new all-time highs. When the whole sector started to lift on the good news flow from the housing sector, Bank of the Internet (BOFI) just went ballistic—from $17 to 46 in a year.

Over time, I noticed that if I hate the stocks that have technically perfect breakouts, the odds are that I have found some great winners. Think about it. The only reason to hate an industry is because of a bias that has been built by the media.

From a sentimental point of view, we want to buy when an asset is ridiculed. For practical purposes, we add a new high as a filter—we want to own them at the right time, so our capital works for us, instead of getting stuck in trendless consolidations or, worse, in positions that go against us.

Why the 52-week High List Is So Important

1. We don't want to be first. We want to be in stocks that move, and being on the 52-week high list attracts a lot of attention.
2. It is an important benchmark, followed by many investors.
3. You cannot make a cent before the market agrees with you. The market's way of agreeing with you is sending your stock to the 52-week high list.

The market is often forward-looking, and it discounts events that have not happened yet. This is why sometimes you will see stocks breaking out on the 52-week high list but you will have no clue what they are doing there. This is a good thing. By the time the reason behind a move is clear to everyone, most of this move will likely be over. This is just how the market works. You could accept it and adjust, or you could look for another field to apply your intellect. Buffett likes to joke that if you have an IQ of 160, you could give away 30 points and you would still be a very successful investor.

The only reason two people perceive the same situation differently is because they have different experience. When you have different experience, you have different expectations and act differently. When a stock or an industry that is widely hated or massively neglected starts making new 52-week highs, someone must be seeing something the majority isn't. It takes real buying power for such a stock to break out to new 52-week highs.

Something must've changed for a stock to hit a new 52-week high. Somebody is buying. We already talked about the notion that the 52-week high list could sometimes be considered a shortcut to the minds of smart people: a place where we can read their investment theses and understand the trends that they are seeing and trying to discount.

If so many people hate the stock and the industry, why are they not impacting its price negatively? The reason is very simple:

- Those who are short are already short. They've already sold with an intention to buy back at lower prices. They have no impact on supply anymore. In fact, past short selling is a source of future demand. The stock is already at new 52-week highs, so most of the short-sellers are likely under water. The first new 52-week high doesn't discourage them. On the contrary, some of them will probably double down and short more. They are the source that will fuel the rally in the future as the stock keeps going persistently higher.

- Those who had been burned by the stock or industry in the past couple years are totally indifferent to what is currently going on. They don't want to hear about it. They don't care. They don't believe. When an asset is down big several years in a row, we could make the rational assumption that almost everyone who wanted to sell has already done so. Those still playing are day and swing traders, who are renters and don't own it for more than a few days. Considering all those factors, it takes only a very little bump in demand for prices to rise. Such a bump that could be caused by two factors:

1. A surprising earnings report or contract that totally changes expectations and perceptions. Prices change when expectations change.
2. Smart people start buying in anticipation of future positive catalysts.

We don't buy stocks that are out of fashion. We buy stocks that are hated and ridiculed and are making new 52-week highs. We don't buy low expectations. We buy bearish sentiment and indifference + rising expectations + new 52-week highs.

Perception is worse than the reality. There is a difference between perceptions and expectations. The former deals with the present, the latter with the future. Our expectations are based on our experience in similar situations. Apparently, people who have been through this recovery process before and understand the cyclical nature of market psychology see potential in this stock and are willing to put their money to work. Otherwise, prices would not be rising. In a situation where there is very little supply, it does not take much demand to lift prices higher:

1. Everyone who wanted to sell and take the loss has already done so.

2. Almost everyone who wanted to go short has done so; therefore, the short interest is over 15%, and the cost of borrowing is extremely high.
3. In such situations, it does not take a lot of demand to push prices higher.

There is a difference between expectations and sentiment. A stock could make a new 52-week high on the basis of the rising expectations of select forward-looking individuals, while the general public doesn't pay attention and is indifferent. A new 52-week high from a proper technical base garnished with negative sentiment is one of the most powerful combinations.

New 52-week highs + outsized skepticism and outright ridicule is a very powerful equity selection combination. The best performing stocks in any single year will have those same characteristics. They will keep going higher, and people will keep making fun of them and even try to short them and say that this is only a short-term blip and the stock is bound to reverse lower. The media won't even pay attention to it. Indifference and low press coverage is good.

Every truth goes through 3 stages: at first it is ridiculed, then it is violently opposed, and, eventually, it is accepted as self-evident. The best-performing stocks in any single year go through those three stages. We want to own them when they are ridiculed and start to gradually scale out when their trend is accepted as given and self-evident. The trend does not end when in the third stage. It accelerates and gets a lot more violent and noticeable. The press coverage increases substantially, and not only from specialized financial papers like IBD, WSJ, Bloomberg, and FT, but also in more mainstream press sources. A trend could continue a lot longer than most people expect. We don't sell an entire position when everyone starts to like it. We start to slowly scale out. We sell 20% here and there for the sake of locking some profit.

If, for some wicked reason, we start seeing on the 52-week high list numerous coal and natural gas stocks, we will know that these are groups to focus on. I am not saying that it will necessarily happen. But if it does, you can bet your dog that I will be very interested.

With this approach, you only need to find one or two industries per year to achieve substantial returns. Focus on where the money is going, and if that place is universally hated and ridiculed, buy as much as your risk management approach allows and make sure you make some real money. It is a philosophy that should serve you well for the rest of your investing life; the more you practice it, the better you will become.

Turnaround Situations Need Catalysts

Price is the ultimate catalyst. Sometimes a widely neglected industry will start making new 52-week highs before the underlying companies report any notable growth. In this case, a few forward-looking people with purchasing power are positioning for a major change, as happened with housing stocks in 2012 and select banks in 2011 (Bank of the Internet, Silicon Valley Bank).

Other times, an unexpected strong earnings report will cause a sudden gap to major new highs, and this will be the beginning of a major turnaround situation, as was the case with Netflix, First Solar, Sunpower, and Green Mountain Coffee Roasters.

Almost all stocks eventually make new 52-week highs in a bull market, including some really crappy businesses, and that new 52-week high would look like a turn-around situation. How do you distinguish between the real turn-around situations, which could deliver 500% return in a year, and the high-flyers that are likely to give back quickly what they have gained? There are two important arguments that I would like to cover here:

1. We could filter by focusing on stocks of companies that have just reported a lot better than expected earnings. We could focus only on stocks that are lifted with their entire industries.

2. What is the difference between a stock going up 300% and then giving back most of it and a stock that appreciated 300% and then stays there for a while? For you as a market participant, it should not matter much. You could make a lot of money in both cases. Every trend eventually comes to an end, but this does not mean that you should give all your gains back.

When a stock that has been a disappointment for a few years suddenly appears on the 52-week high list, it will attract a lot of attention. If stock that only a few months ago was the butt of jokes in the investors' community suddenly starts making new highs—this is huge news. Most people will be extremely skeptical, but this is exactly what you want to see in a trend. Every trend needs skeptics and disbelievers; otherwise, there won't be anyone left to buy. Why do people hate this kind of stock? The answer is very simple: it has underperformed and disappointed for a pro-longed period of time. The media has written a ton of negative articles about it. In a way, the perception has become worse than the reality. The worst-case scenario has been discounted. Remember that the market tends to over-discount identified risks. This is one explanation why stocks that are dropped from the Nasdaq 100 during the end of the year rebalancing tend to outperform the next year. The stocks that are dropped are always among the worst performers of the current year. Many funds sell them for tax loss purposes to a point that they become a bargain for value-hunting investors. The removal from the Nasdaq 100 is the crescendo of a bad year—an event that could only be described as sell the rumors, buy the news.

Sentiment Cycle In A Typical Turnaround Situation

All stocks are price-cyclical. Upside and downside momentum beyond three years often leads to mean-reversion, especially when it comes to whole sectors and industries.

The way most people react to price action is very similar, and it has not altered since the existing of equity markets. It has not changed because human psychology has remained static. This is why the same patterns repeat over and over again.

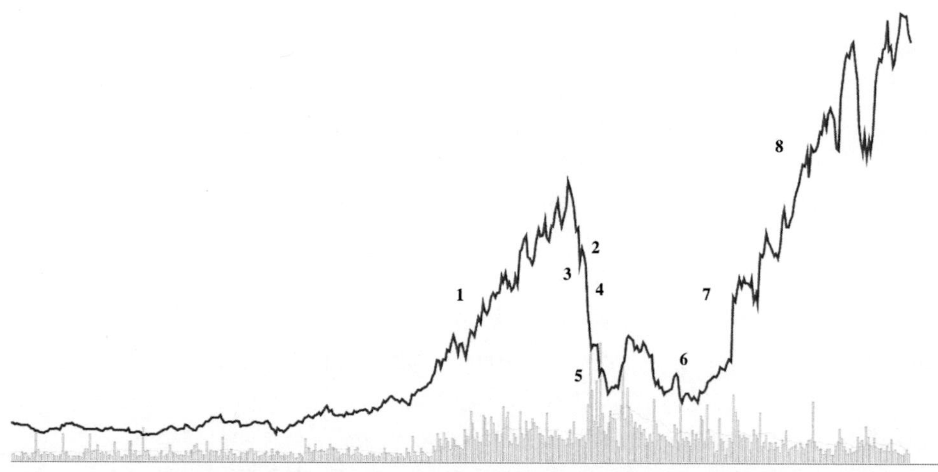

1. Nice steady uptrend. Everyone loves the industry.
2. The trend is over.
3. Knife catchers are getting slaughtered.
4. There are very few buyers. Momentum guys are out or short. Value guys are not interested. Everyone rushes through the exit.
5. People are making fun of the industry. It is "dead" for good.

6. Indifference. No one cares about it. If it is mentioned, it is to make fun of it. Everyone agrees that it has no future. The stage of indifference could last anywhere between a few months to a few quarters. It will also be reflected in the smaller trading volume and number of analysts that follow the group.
7. Point of interest. It suddenly makes a new multi-month high on relatively big volume.
8. Many will not believe this move and will fight on the way up, creating conditions for further short squeeze. Many will be afraid to enter, because "it is up too much, too fast."

There's a small but very important detail here. You don't go and buy all stocks that are down 90% in the past three years. You wait for a new 52-week high or at least new 50-day highs from a proper base on huge volume before you go long. Having a fundamental catalyst like a big earnings surprise behind a breakout to new 52-week highs improves substantially the odds of finding a big winner.

A dog can remain a dog a lot longer than most people expect. Remember the new 52-week high requirement. Without it, nothing else matters. We want price momentum on our side. We want price to confirm our thesis.

Some people like to say that they look to buy low expectations, not low prices, but keep in mind that low expectations are not a catalyst. They are just a measure of the potential move once a real catalyst is presented. P/E and price action don't necessarily measure expectations. Expectations are measured by sentiment. Different people have different expectations due to different backgrounds and market philosophies.

What we want is an asset that separates the opinion. Consensus opinions are dangerous and often already discounted. The obvious rarely happens, but the unexpected constantly occurs. We want stocks that are rising in price and on which analysts totally disagree. At the early stages of Tesla Motors' appreciation, analysts had no idea how to value it. The range in analysts' projections was 15 billion, which was as much as what the company was worth at the time. These are characteristics of a stock that deserves our special attention.

We look for an upside move (new 52-week high) in a previously neglected stock that is so surprising that no one believes it. Such setup means two things:

1. Early longs are eager to sell early and pocket profits; if this initial buying pressure could not hold the stock of interest and it continues to go higher, this is a clear indication that someone with a lot of purchasing power is accumulating.

2. New short-sellers start to appear.

In early 2013, I wrote that solar stocks will be to 2013 what housing-related stocks were to 2012—the best performers coming from a place no one expects. I did not believe enough in my arguments, so I was an early seller and I traded in and out of the solar names, rather than holding them for a longer period of time. In strong trending markets, the sitting with your big winners is what makes you the most money. In low-volatility, trending markets, you will regret selling too early. In high-volatility, mean-reversion markets, you will regret not selling earlier.

The lesson: the best-performing stocks in any given year often come from industries that no one expects. Be open-minded. When you see widely disliked stocks breaking out to new 52-week highs from perfect technical bases, buy some. When you buy and people make fun of you, make sure to buy some more. When someone you consider very smart tells you that you are crazy for buying them, go and buy some more. Having people disagreeing with your investment thesis while your stocks are making new 52-week highs is the most beautiful thing that could happen to you. Every trend needs skeptics and doubters; otherwise, there wouldn't be anyone left to buy.

You Cannot Achieve Big Returns By Following The Conventional Wisdom

They say that two types of people are the most dangerous in the stock market: those who know nothing and those who act like they know everything. The more important question is, who are the types of people that make the most money in the stock market? I would say they are those who have a very good understanding of how markets work and those who end up being right about something about which the majority of people are wrong.

If you want to achieve outsized returns, you have to do something that most people are not willing to do. If something feels psychologically difficult to do in the stock market, it is often the right thing to do. If it were easy, everyone would do it, and therefore the end result would not be anything spectacular.

Doing something that is psychologically difficult does not guarantee you success, but it does guarantee you outsized returns if you end up being right. The only way to make big money is to be right about something about which almost everyone else is wrong. If you are right about something about which everyone else is right, you will only achieve average returns. Sometimes being average is not a bad outcome, but we are striving for more than that, right?

What are some of the signs that other people are not on the same page as you? They will tell you. Your idea will seem so ridiculous to them that they will make fun of it. You know what? This is a really good sign. It means that you are onto something big. It means that if you are right, your payback will be huge. Being a contrarian doesn't always work, but when it does the payoff is ginormous.

You cannot make big money conventionally. If all believe that an asset is a great buy, then their beliefs are very likely to be already reflected in the price of this asset. Everyone already owns it. If almost everyone believes that an asset is a terrible buy and it yet makes a new 52-week high, it is probably well worth our consideration.

If you catch yourself not wanting to take a new 52-week high because of what you have heard in the media, the odds are that you have encountered a big future winner. Many other investors have probably been brainwashed the same way you were, and this is why everyone is skeptical when the stock of interest makes new highs. The existence of pessimists is needed for the durability of trends.

Every trend needs skeptics and doubters; otherwise there won't be anyone left to buy. This is why I always smile when I see people making fun of or questioning my investment ideas. It tells me that I am probably on the right path.

I have a very clear rule of thumb: any time I see a perfect technical setup and I catch myself not wanting to buy the stock, because of personal, irrational biases (I don't like the company, the management, the industry), I force myself to take the position. I know that the odds are good that I am onto something great. This is how investing works. It has to be a little counter-intuitive.

In his book *The Most Important Thing*, Howard Marks teaches us:

> *"When everyone believes something is risky, their unwillingness to buy usually reduces its price to the point where it's not risky at all.*

> *Broadly negative opinion can make it the least risky thing, since all optimism has been driven out of its price."*

Mr. Marks looks at contrarianism from a value point of view. I like to view contrarianism from a momentum point of view. I assume (I have never done it), it is really hard for many people to buy an asset when it is down 90% from its highs and it has kept going down for many months and even years. Or maybe, it is easier, because it seems cheaper. What I know is that it is always an emotional struggle to buy a stock when it is up 100% in the past six months and it is at all-time highs. And yet, this is exactly how many multi-year leaders begin the journey of their super-performance.

No one has ever made a killing by going with the consensus opinion, but there are many people who have lost their fortunes by going against the crowd. Our goal is not to be contrarian for the sake of being contrarians. We do it with only one intention: to make money.

There is a huge difference between thinking contrarian and acting contrarian. The latter is a lot harder to implement because it goes against human nature. More often than not, being a contrarian means staying with the price trend; it means buying a stock when it makes new 52-week highs and it comes from an industry most are afraid to touch.

Chapter 7
There Is Always A Silver Lining

"It is not entirely clear what causes deep market corrections, but without them many of the best performing long-term investors would have never achieved their spectacular returns." – Peter Lynch

A Glass Half Full, But With What?

Why is it always 30% chance of rain and never 70% chance of sun? Blame it on the weathermen, but this is a good example of how our society decodes new information. We are biologically wired to pay more attention to scary headlines, and as a result the media bombards us with pessimism.

Somehow the mainstream press always finds a way to put a negative spin on every piece of economic data. If retail sales are down, the consumer is not buying, and the economy might be entering recession. If retail sales are up, there is a threat of inflation. If oil prices rise too fast, it is bad for the economy because it will diminish the purchasing power of the consumer. If oil prices fall too quickly, it is a sign of a slowing economy. What is wrong with these people?

In 2014, Russian news site City Reporter decided to perform a social experiment. They reported only good news for an entire day. They only featured positive stories and gave silver linings to all negative stories. For example, they ran a story entitled "No disruption on roads despite snow." The results were catastrophic for the website's traffic. The City Reporter lost two-thirds of its normal readership that day.

At the end of the day, the majority of journalists and media people are interested in catching people's attention. An article with a warning and negative spin on any news does a great job achieving that, but it is rarely a good source of investment advice. Ignore grandiose negative headlines. Wildly optimistic headlines could be just as dangerous, but this is a topic for another discussion.

There is a better way to look at the world and think deeply about your investments. I call it "the glass half full" approach. By no means is it an approach that is based on wishful thinking and day-dreaming. It comes from a simple understanding of how markets function. Every company's rising cost is another company's rising revenue. And the opposite is also true: every company's declining revenue is another company's declining cost. And do you know what the best part is? The stock market usually does a good job of recognizing the beneficiaries in every situation by sending their stocks to the 52-week high list. Take advantage of it.

Money Never Sleeps

Every crisis brings an opportunity. Every bust in one area of financial markets puts the foundations for a boom in another area. Money never sleeps. It constantly goes somewhere—sometimes, because of rational reasons, but other times, because of sheer speculation. Nevertheless, as long as humans are involved in financial markets, there will be booms and busts, crises and recoveries.

America went into recession in the early 2000s, and Americans went to school to gain another diploma. As a result, education stocks rallied to the sky. Between 2000 and 2004, shares of Apollo Education went from $10 to $100.

Terrorists hit the Twin Towers in 2001, and America went to war. As a result, defense stocks appreciated substantially. Between 2002 and 2005, shares of Kevlar® makers Ceradyne went up 1800%.

The bust in tech stocks in the early 2000s alienated regular Americans from stocks, and they decided to put their money into houses. Homebuilders' stocks went up five times and more in a fairly short period of time, before they went bust. Between 2001 and 2005, shares of Beazer Homes went from $40 to $370, Toll Brothers went from $7 to $50, Ryland Group went from $7 to $80, etc.

The Fed's aggressive monetary easing coupled with emerging markets' hunger for basic materials caused a massive spike in demand and inflation. As a result, commodities went through the roof. While market averages deteriorated in the first half of 2008, many basic material stocks quadrupled. Yes, in the second half of 2008, they gave up most of their profits and then some more, but they created incredible opportunities for people who were simply following price trends and had an exit strategy. Between 2007 and mid-2008, shares of potash maker Mosaic went from $15 to $150.

The financial crisis of 2008–2009 brought all stocks down on their knees. Many small caps were priced for bankruptcy. Most of them survived and went up more than 1000% in the ensuing four to five years. Mattress maker Select Comfort was trading near 25 cents per share in early 2009. In early 2015, it is trading near $35. Big corrections create the opportunity for big recoveries.

The European sovereign bond crisis of 2011 and the overall slow employment recovery in the United States encouraged the Federal Reserve to launch a series of unprecedented monetary policy injections with the code name "Quantitative Easing." Waves of capital flooded public and private markets and caused material appreciation in most financial assets.

Embrace Market Corrections

We live in times of perpetual booms and busts that come one after another. In fact, they cause each other. Every five years or so, there is a deep market pullback that creates incredible opportunities for savvy investors. Corrections make investors a lot of money. Most of them just don't know it at the time. And I do not refer only to value investors, who are happy to buy high-quality businesses and distressed assets on the cheap. I also refer to momentum and growth investors.

In the fall of 2008, it felt like the financial world as we know it was going to end. Stocks were plunging every day, hit by waves of forced liquidation. Institutions were selling not because they wanted to, but because they had to, due to redemptions from clients and margin calls. Individual investors were scrambling to exit their shares at any price. They just wanted to be in cash. Who's to blame them? Companies that were considered indestructible filed for bankruptcy or their stocks collapsed more than 50%. People were scared and did not trust anyone.

In the midst of the biggest financial crisis since the Great Depression, Warren Buffett wrote an article published in the *New York Times* titled "Buy American. I Am." When volatility and correlations were at record-high levels, when most investors were running scared and could not sell their stocks fast enough, Buffett was buying with both hands. Buffett was early. Stocks continued to decline for five more months and went a lot lower before they finally bottomed in March 2009. At that time, many stocks, especially small caps, were priced for bankruptcy, which never materialized. In the following five years, stocks staged a massive rally. Quite a few went up 1000% or more. The beauty of the stock market is that you never have to be first in order to make a lot of money. In March 2009, you did not have to guess which stocks were going go survive in order to profit from their recovery. You could have achieved substantial returns by entering in the middle of their trends, when their existence was not questionable and when they were breaking out to new 52-week highs from proper bases.

Do you remember the first stocks to hit new all-time highs after the bottom in March 2009? As the major market indexes were making new lows every day in February and early March of 2009, a select group of stocks like Netflix, Keurig Green Mountain, and AutoZone were trading tightly near their all-time high levels. As soon as the indexes bounced, those three stocks made new all-time highs. They ended up becoming some of the best performers in the first two years of the market recovery.

Patterns repeat like clockwork in financial markets. The only things that change are the names of the stocks that form them. What happened with Netflix and Green Mountain in 2009 has happened in every single correction in market history:

1. Stocks that show relative strength during major market pullbacks become the leaders of the next rally.
2. The first stocks that break out to new 52-week highs after a correction often outperform substantially during the recovery.

Let's take a look at a few examples from the most recent market corrections.

When Is The Absolute Best Time To Buy Stocks

You don't have to be in the market all the time or to watch closely every tick. In fact, if you do – it would be very counter-productive and potentially dangerous for your returns. It is hard for professional money managers not to be active, because their clients almost demand it—as if being more active is positively correlated with higher returns. No, it is not. In fact, it is often the opposite. But being active is often interpreted as working hard. In markets, it is more important to work smart, not hard. Less is more. Most people will do incredibly well if they are active only four to five times a year and let their winners run long enough to make a difference. The best time to get aggressive and put money to work is right after a market correction.

The most money is made at the beginning and the end of a bull market, because no one believes the moves. At the beginning, the fear of losing is stronger than the fear of missing out. At the end, most people think that it is too good to be true, and short-sellers are forced to cover their bets.

Warren Buffett likes to say that he is greedy when the majority of others are fearful and fearful when the majority is greedy. Guess when people are most fearful? Right after the market indexes have had a quick 10–15% correction and every post in the financial press is about doom and gloom.

Some of the biggest money-making opportunities in the stock market will come right after a big selloff. It is then that the risk is lowest and the potential rewards are highest. The best time to buy stocks is after a >10% market correction. Sounds easy, but it is a lot harder in practice. After a >10% market correction, most people are scared and think only about capital protection. The fear of losing is a lot bigger than the fear of missing out. Almost everyone hates stocks and is afraid of holding them for more than a few days. Corrections often last long enough to condition most people to sell their winners quickly. As a result, very few make any real money at the beginning stage of market recoveries.

It pays to be aggressive when others are afraid, but also keep in mind that once in a while a 10% correction turns into a 50% bear market. No one could know with any kind of certainty when the end of a correction and the beginning of a new rally is.

Here is a good rule of thumb.

The end of most market corrections is typically marked by breadth divergence. There is a divergence when an index makes new correction lows, while a smaller number of its underlying stocks make new lows. For example, let assume that the S & P 500 is down 10% from its highs, and there are 100 stocks that are making new 52-week lows. If the S & P 500 continues lower and its pullback reaches, let's say 14%, while the number of stocks making new 52-week lows decreases to 70, we have a divergence. The existence of a divergence is not enough to start buying heavily. Bottoms are not formed by excessive selling. They are formed by strong buying. You also need to see stocks that are breaking out to new 50-day or 52-week highs before you become more aggressive in your capital allocation.

Now that we know when it is really a good time to buy, we should address the question of what to buy.

Relative Strength

The biggest market "secret" is that from a long-term perspective, it has always been a "market of stocks" with very fat tails in both ends of the performance spectrum. The first stocks to make new 52-week highs after a six- to 12-week correction are usually the ones that will outperform significantly over the next two to six months.

The silver lining of every correction is that it makes the spotting of future winners a lot easier. When markets correct, future leaders consolidate and form bases with incredible risk/reward prospects. During corrections, it is important to pay attention to stocks that exhibit relative strength.

Relative strength is very simple to spot: look for stocks that go sideways while the indexes drop significantly. During corrections, correlations often go to 1.00, meaning that most stocks move up and down together, regardless of their individual merits. If a stock manages to hold its ground and consolidate through time or even make an attempt to make a new high, it is likely being accumulated by institutions. Because of the nature of their size, many institutions prefer to buy on pullbacks and during market corrections, which provide liquidity to mask their accumulation. Once the pressure from the general market is removed, those stocks tend to outperform.

Relative strength is a powerful equity selection tool, but it could be very misleading at the beginning stages of a correction. In a real correction, almost all stocks decline. Those that break out to new 52-week highs as the market averages start to deteriorate often quickly reverse lower. As they say, from failed moves come fast moves. The concept of relative strength adds a lot more value after the major indexes decline 7–10% or more.

If you remember only one principle from this book, it should be the concept of relative strength. Market pullbacks of at least 7–10% happen every single year. During that time, there are always stocks that consolidate sideways or try to make new 52-week highs while the averages plummet. These are the stocks to which you want to pay special attention. These are the stocks that you want to own heavily when the indexes bounce. These are the stocks that are very likely to become the next market leaders and go up 50–100% in the three to nine months after the correction. These are the stocks that could make a real difference in your returns.

NFLX Netflix, Inc. Nasdaq GS
©StockCharts.com
31-Mar-2009 Open 39.51 High 43.97 Low 39.05 Close 42.92 Volume 4.6M Chg +3.24 (+8.17%)
SPY 70.46 (31 Mar)
NFLX (Weekly) 42.92 (31 Mar)
new 52-week high while market is crashing
it goes up 650% in the next 2 years
2008 Feb Mar Apr May Jun Jul Aug Sep Oct Nov Dec 2009 Feb Mar

GMCR Keurig Green Mountain, Inc. Nasdaq GS
©StockCharts.com
31-Mar-2009
Open 10.17 High 10.73 Low 9.92 Close 10.52 Volume 5.7M Chg +0.19 (+1.80%)
SPY 70.46 (31 Mar)
GMCR (Weekly) 10.52 (31 Mar)
consolidates sideways while market is crashing
goes up 1000% in the following 2 years
Jun
Jul
Aug
Sep
Oct
Nov
Dec
2009
Feb
Mar

AZO Autozone Inc. Nevada NYSE
©StockCharts.com
31-Mar-2009 Open 162.60 High 165.21 Low 160.75 Close 162.62 Volume 1.8M Chg -1.57 (-0.96%)
SPY 70.46 (31 Mar)
AZO (Weekly) 162.62 (31 Mar)
new all-time high while the market is crashing
it goes up 350% in the next 5 years
Jun
Jul
Aug
Sep
Oct
Nov
Dec
2009
Feb
Mar

PCYC Pharmacyclics, Inc. Nasdaq GM
©StockCharts.com
30-Nov-2011
Open 13.00 High 15.34 Low 12.90 Close 15.23 Volume 4.6M Chg +2.54 (+20.02%)
SPY 116.39 (30 Nov)
125
120
116.39
110
105
PCYC (Weekly) 15.23 (30 Nov)
15.23
14
13
12
11
10
9
8
7
6
5
consolidates through time while market is crashing
as soon as the market bounces,
goes up 500% in the next 14 months
2011
Feb
Mar
Apr
May
Jun
Jul
Aug
Sep
Oct
Nov

QIHU QIHOO 360 Technology Co. Ltd. NYSE
© StockCharts.com
30-Nov-2012 Open 23.54 High 25.45 Low 22.67 Close 24.99 Volume 10.3M Chg +1.56 (+6.66%)
SPY 135.21 (30 Nov)
about 8% mkt correction
QIHU (Weekly) 24.99 (30 Nov)
goes up 380% in the next 14 months
Feb Mar Apr May Jun Jul Aug Sep Oct Nov

QLYS Qualys, Inc. Nasdaq GS
©StockCharts.com
31-Oct-2014 Open 28.25 High 32.18 Low 28.08 Close 32.08 Volume 1.4M Chg +3.75 (+13.24%)
SPY 199.66 (31 Oct)
almost 10% pullback
QLYS (Weekly) 32.08 (31 Oct)
new high
goes to $50 in the next 4 months
2014
Feb
Mar
Apr
May
Jun
Jul
Aug
Sep
Oct

AGIO Agios Pharmaceuticals, Inc. Nasdaq GS
©StockCharts.com
17-Oct-2014
Open 61.19 High 69.98 Low 59.78 Close 64.27 Volume 4.5M Chg +3.39 (+5.57%)
SPY 186.60 (17 Oct)
AGIO (Weekly) 64.27 (17 Oct)
doubles in the next 2 months
2014
Feb
Mar
Apr
May
Jun
Jul
Aug
Sep
Oct

Chapter 8
Sooner Or Later, Every Trend Ends

"It is not important whether we are right or wrong, but how much money we make when we are right and how much we lose, when we are wrong." – George Soros

"We are in the business of making mistakes. The only difference between the winners and the losers is that the winners make small mistakes, while the losers make big mistakes."- Ned Davis

Buy and Hold Is Not As Easy As It Sounds

You have probably heard some form of the following stories a thousand times:

Had you invested $10,000 in Starbucks at the day of its IPO in 1992, you would be sitting on about $1.4 million today (early 2015).

If you had been brave enough to invest $10,000 in Priceline when it was a five-dollar stock in 2001, you would be sitting on $1.8 million today.

If you had invested $10,000 in Cisco Systems in 1990, you would have $6.7 million today.

Hindsight bias makes investing seem a lot easier than it is. Pointing out winners of the past could be a futile exercise if you don't realize the limitations of studying historical returns. What no one will tell you is that holding those stocks through their pullbacks was excruciatingly hard. For each Priceline, Cisco Systems, and Starbucks, there were hundreds of others that looked promising at the beginning stage of their price appreciation but failed to deliver positive long-term returns.

Any consistently successful investor will tell you that the secret behind accumulating wealth in the stock market is to cut your losers short and let your winners run. Anyone can buy a stock. Not everyone can hold a stock long enough to make a difference in his or her returns. Holding is hard.

If you spend enough time investing, eventually you will realize that the three smartest words in the field are "Never say never." All big long-term winners go through deep pullbacks that challenge the conviction of even the most loyal shareholders. It is not easy to see your favorite stock go down 50% or 90%, no matter how much money you made in it in the past.

Let me give you a quick riddle in risk management. Let's say you invest $10,000 in a stock with great growth potential. It goes up 1000% in the next two years, but then a bear market comes and hits all stocks. Your stock corrects 90%. How much is your investment worth after the correction? Exactly $10,000. If you simply bought and held, you would have as much money as you did when you began. I don't know about you, but I don't think this return is very appealing.

Some trends last more than a decade and deliver thousands of percent return. Some trends last only a few quarters and fizzle after a 200–300% move. The truth is that sooner or later, every trend ends. Some stocks manage to recover after a 50% pullback, make new 52-week highs, and offer good secondary buy opportunities. Many simply never recover from their big drawdowns or take a very, very long time to do so.

Buy and hold forever rarely works. The market graveyard is full of trends that last only a few quarters. The best performing stocks in any given year are very volatile and not for the faint of heart.

Let's take a look at a few examples:

Yelp shares went from $20 to $100 in 2013; then they declined 50%.

Go Pro shares went from $30 to $100 in about three months in 2014. Then they plunged 50%.

Pandora shares went from $10 to $37 in 2013 through early 2014. Then they dropped 70%.

Bitauto Holdings shares went from $5 to $100 in two years. Then they dropped 50% in three months.

It is typical for story/momentum stocks to go up several hundred percentage points in a short period of time and then give back > 50% of their move.

YELP Yelp Inc. NYSE
©StockCharts.com
27-Mar-2015
Open 44.86 High 47.36 Low 44.74 Close 47.16 Volume 12.0M Chg +2.22 (+4.94%)
YELP (Weekly) 47.16
47.16
J J A S O N D 13 F M A M J J A S O N D 14 F M A M J J A S O N D 15 F M

GPRO GoPro, Inc. Nasdaq GS
©StockCharts.com
27-Mar-2015
Open 40.30 High 44.34 Low 39.81 Close 42.70 Volume 31.0M Chg +2.30 (+5.69%)
GPRO (Weekly) 42.70
42.70
Jun Jul Aug Sep Oct Nov Dec 2015 Feb Mar

If we know that the trends of most high-growth momentum stocks last only several quarters and they experience tremendous drawdowns, why should we even bother with them as an asset class? Because we could make a lot of money in them. Their trends might end, but this doesn't mean that we have to give back most of the gains that they deliver.

Not every hot stock today will turn into a long-term winner. Most will turn out to be short-term fads. With some basic risk management skills, you could still make a lot of money in them.

There are things that we know we know. There are things that we know we don't know. There are also things that we don't know we don't know. The biggest investment risks are usually in the third group.

We don't know which stocks will actually become huge long-term winners. We don't know how long a trend will last.

We know what is a good entry point from a risk to reward perspective. We know how much we risk, how much we allocate, where we will add to our positions, and why we will exit. That's all we need to know in order to consistently make money.

What are some of the things we don't know we don't know? Weird question, right? For most people it is about their empathy gap.

Empathy Gap

One of my favorite movie quotes ever is from the movie *Batman Begins*: "It is not who you are underneath that defines you. It is what you do." This quote describes perfectly the biggest obstacle for most investors and the main reason why there is a distance between desired and actual results. Empathy gap is the main cause behind most trading and investing mistakes. Empathy gap is the difference between how you believe you will act under certain circumstances and how you actually act when the time comes.

Do you think you will remain calm in the face of a 50% decline in one or several of your holdings and you will ride them back to new all-time highs? Think again. Most people will give up and sell in the face of such big losses. You have to plan for your inherent human weaknesses. You need to have a clear strategy that will your protect profits and confidence.

Maybe Your Goal Should Not Be To Find The Next Apple

Maybe your goal should not be to find stocks that will go up 2000% in 20 years. Warren Buffett likes to marry his stocks and ride them through good and bad till death do them apart. His approach is not for everyone. A much better approach for you might be to aim at stocks that could go up 100% to 500% in six to 24 months and sell them as they violate their uptrends.

Finding stocks that have the potential to be the next Apple is easy only in hindsight. The truth is that no one could know for sure. If you could go back in time and tell Steve Jobs and Tim Cook how successful Apple would become, they would probably think you were crazy. Even they had no idea in the early 2000s.

Very few of today's leaders will turn into the next Apple. The few that do will have incredibly volatile paths along the way. Riding those trends through their inevitable > 50% drawdowns will make the holding part pretty much impossible for most people. The good news is that there will be thousands of mini-Apples in your life as an investor—thousands of stocks that will go up 100% to 500% in a year or two. Anyone could catch 10 or 20 of them.

Some trends last several months and others several years, but eventually they all end. This is not an opinion. It is a fact. The goal of investing is to keep your profits when the inevitable correction comes.

Why Trends End

Trends end when expectations change. Expectations could change for various reasons:

1. Weakness in the general market.

All stocks are price cyclical. A company could triple its earnings and still lose 50% of its market cap in a bear market. Sentiment trumps fundamentals in the short-term perspective.

Violent market corrections often lead to panic selling. During periods of forced liquidations and redemptions, all stocks suffer. Forced liquidation means "get me out at any price." Even the stocks of the most solid businesses suffer in such periods.

2. No company could sustain high expectations forever.

Anything priced for perfection eventually disappoints. The cause for a letdown could be missing earnings expectations, but this is not always the case. The stock market is forward-looking and it discounts proactively, which means that price trends often start and end before earnings growth trends reverse.

Many trends have good fundamental basis. They are based on rational expectations. The market is forward-looking, but it is constantly looking for feedback, in terms of positive growth data. If it does not receive it, it re-evaluates its initial thesis and start to correct. A good story could only get you so far.

At some point, people wake up from their dream. They sober up and realize that not only have they discounted a future that is never going to materialize (at least not soon), but they could actually lose money if they keep holding their position. Many smart people like to take partial profits on strength. At some point, their supply overwhelms the underlying demand, which causes a huge counter-trend range expansion. There comes a big down day or week. All of a sudden, more people realize that they are not untouchable and that buying should not be mindless. The fear of losing gradually overwhelms the fear of missing out.

Trends last because the market tends to over-discount identified risks and opportunities, until one day it realizes that the perception and the reality are miles away and there's no chance of them aligning anytime soon. Corrections happen not necessarily because the market is discounting some future event. Sometimes they happen because the market is correcting a previously incorrect view.

3. Valuation Eventually Matters

Sometimes the market will give the benefit of the doubt to a company with great growth potential, and it will discount a bright future. Not all companies will live up to the expectation. At some point, the market will realize that it has been wrong all along, and it will correct itself. Investors will wake up from their sweet dreams, and suddenly the fear of losing will trump the fear of missing out. When this happens, look out below.

When growth stocks are in an uptrend, valuation does not matter, because the people who invest in them don't buy or sell for valuation reasons. It is all about sentiment, expectations, and EPS/sales growth. Some short-sellers fade growth names on valuation reasons alone, but they could be wrong for 300%, before they are right for a 50% pullback.

Valuation matters when market mood shifts from complacency and euphoria to doom and gloom. One of the ways to gauge sentiment shift is to watch the market reaction to earnings reports. When the market reacts poorly to what appears to be "good news" on the surface, consider it a major sign that the trend might be over or at least a reminder that the easy money in the trend has already been made.

Valuation matters once an uptrend is broken and a stock starts to slide. A stock could go up 500% in a year and then lose 50% of it in a couple months. A correction usually comes a lot slower than everyone expects, and when it happens, it develops a lot faster than anyone expects. Growth stocks often take the stairwell up and an elevator down. The decline is more furious, because there is no one to support them on the way down. When a momentum stock appreciates, it climbs a constant wall of worry. Skepticism slowly dissipates until that stock accelerates its momentum and forces all short sellers to cover their bets. In this stage, a typical momentum stock will go parabolic. It could run 50% in a couple weeks or less. Such momentum spikes are used by smart investors and institutions to unload some or all of their shares. Institutions need liquidity in order to establish large enough positions. This is why they prefer to buy individual stocks on pullbacks or during general market corrections that send all stocks lower. Institutions also need liquidity in order to sell their large positions. That liquidity often comes from:

A) Short-sellers who receive margin calls and are forced to cover their bets.
B) Late-comers who chase and enter a momentum stock very late in its price cycle—for example, after it has appreciated 300% in the past year and it is very extended from its latest technical base. In this case, the fear of missing out trumps the fear of losing.

Why do most momentum stocks decline so much after they peak? Because there is no one to support them. People who bought on the way up are either out or short. Value investors don't even touch those stocks; The market is very likely to over-react to the downside if it had overreacted to the upside before. It is like pushing a swing: the stronger you push in one direction, the stronger it comes back to you.

4. An Increase In Supply

A) Many companies use their stock as a currency. They could print as much as they want, and many do—to pay their employees and management and to buy competitors. This is why most companies' shares outstanding increase over time.

B) If the company's management doesn't screw it up, Wall Street will. Wall Street is a tireless printing press and a sophisticated distribution and marketing machine. It is in the business of printing stocks that are under demand by the market.

When a company is hot, two things happen: management calls a banker or a banker calls management. If the company is already public, the call is for a potential secondary offering. If the company is still private, the call is for an IPO. More shares in one stock category impacts negatively the supply/demand dynamics. Overstuffing the IPO pipeline is very similar to creating excess capacity. Eventually, it puts downward pressure on prices.

Wall Street's job is to print as much paper to satisfy the most people at exactly the wrong time. All trends end the same way: too many shares distributed to far too many people.

As investors, we have to focus on the positive. Yes, all trends eventually end, but while they last, they could deliver substantial returns. We just have to know when to enter and when to exit.

The Three Pillars Of Risk Management

1. Proper equity selection, which includes timing. Safety is derived from proper timing. Timing is not everything, but it is of crucial importance. We aim to own stocks with potential for substantial and quick price appreciation. We also aim to enter them at a spot that will put us at an immediate profit, which will allow us to go through normal market pullbacks. If we end up being wrong, it will allow us to exit at a small, manageable loss.

2. Having an exit strategy—when to take a loss and when to take profits.

3. Diversification (includes position sizing).

Equity Selection

The father of value investing, Benjamin Graham, will tell you to look for stocks with margins of safety—that is, stocks that are worth more when liquidated than they are currently priced in the market. The theory of margin of safety is simply not applicable for most of today's markets. It was created during the Great Depression when the market was full of stocks trading below their liquid assets' market price. Nowadays, this rarely happens, if ever.

Graham's favorite student, Warren Buffett, advises to look for sustainable advantage. What would be the damage to your business if someone invested a billion dollars to create a competition? If the damage is likely to be minor, it is likely a good business to own for the long term.

My own definition of safety is very different. I believe that safety is derived more from the proper timing of my entries and exits than from the quality of the underlying company. All stocks are price-cyclical. The stock prices of the strongest U.S. corporations have experienced deeper than 50% drawdowns during big market corrections. Most people cannot stomach such drawdowns, and they will probably sell when they get scared, which often happens near the lows.

Warren Buffett's business partner, Charlie Munger, says that if you are not able to stomach a 50% drawdown in your investment holdings, then you are probably not fit to take advantage of the rewards that long-term investing brings.

There has to be a different way to approach this issue. First of all, not all stocks will eventually come back to their highs, or it might take a very long time for them to do so. Second of all, if you are a small individual investor, there is no reason to let your capital holdings depreciate 50%. When you incur a 50% loss, you will need a 100% gain just to break even. This is a lot of work. Why not work smarter rather than harder? Why not cut your losses when they are small (up to 10%) and in the process protect your confidence? Protecting your confidence during market correction is just as important as protecting your capital. If you lose your confidence due to a large number of oversized losses, you won't be in the right psychological state to take advantage of a market rally when it arrives. This would be a terrible thing to happen.

My equity selection takes the following criteria into account, ranked in terms of importance

1. A breakout to new 50-day high or 52-week high from a great technical base.

   A) A breakout helps my timing immensely. It assures that I put money to work in a fast-moving asset. Opportunity cost is important to me. I'd like to allocate money to stocks that are likely to move in my favor immediately after my entry. If the general market is strong, I might buy in expectations of a breakout.

B) A great technical base clearly defines my stop. If this level is breached, then I am wrong. I accept it, take my losses, and go to hunt for other stocks. There are no hard feelings. There are plenty of fish in the sea.

2. It has catalysts I understand. It either belongs to a currently hot industry or it has strong earnings and sales growth. It is even better if it has both.

Exit Strategy – When To Take Profits And How To Keep Losses Small

If you don't know why you buy a stock, you won't know where to exit. If price action is the reason for your purchase, price action should be the reason to sell.

What are some of the reasons to take partial profits or to entirely liquidate a position?

1. Poor reaction to good news.

The market is forward-looking, because everyone tries to be one move ahead of the rest. Prices change when expectations change. By the time expectations are confirmed or disconfirmed by facts (news or earnings reports), most of the move might be already over. If you are waiting for the comfort of good news to buy or for bad news to tell you when to exit, you will always be behind the curve in the investing game.

When a stock reacts negatively to what appears to be good earnings report on the surface, take note. There is a major change in sentiment, which often puts an end to the underlying price trend.

Price trends often start and end before earnings trends. Take for example, the case of Cirrus Logic, which is a major supplier to Apple. When CRUS destroyed earnings estimates in November 2012, many people were shocked to see the market reaction—a gap down from $41 to $37. At the time, the gap was perceived as a buying opportunity by many, citing the spectacular earnings growth. By June 2013, Cirrus was trading near $17 per share. Surprises often follow the direction of the established trend, until in the end. Knowing when that elusive end could be is extremely useful. Poor reaction to what is perceived to be a good earnings report is usually one of the first signs that the price trend is over, and since the price is the only thing that pays us, it is the main trend to which we should pay attention.

2. Distribution

George Soros says that short-term volatility tends to rise at turning points. Look for sudden high-volume, large range-expansion daily or weekly moves against the established trend. For example, a stock that declines 5% in a day above its average daily volume is probably under distribution. I have two simple definitions for distribution:

A) Institutional selling. Institutions are taking profits or need capital to allocate it to other assets. Institutional money is not necessarily the smartest money, but its size has the ability to move stocks – to start and to end trends. It is unwise not to pay attention to it.

B) Transfer of ownership, often from strong to weak hands, from people who are looking to lock in profits in extended names to people who are chasing out of greed and fear of missing out. Why do I call the buyers here weak hands? Because when you chase and buy a stock that is too extended from its late technical base, you put yourself in a very vulnerable position. High-growth

> momentum stocks don't go up every day. They experience normal pullbacks along their uptrend. Not if but when such pullback happens, people who chased will be left under water. What do people who are in a losing position often do? They hope to sell at break-even prices. Even if their stock bounces, it will add to their selling pressure, which is likely to accelerate its downtrend.

When distribution days start to be frequent, chasing is not so mindless anymore. Most people realize that they could actually lose money, which changes their behavior entirely. The fear of losing starts to trump the fear of missing out.

3. Reaching Severely Overbought Levels – When Weekly RSI Goes Above 80

Reaching those levels is usually a good spot to take partial profits. RSI is a simple technical tool, offered by every charting platform.

The technical term "overbought" basically means acceleration in buying to levels that might not be sustainable for too long. What could possible be wrong about an overwhelming number of buyers? It might be an indication that there is no one left to buy. Some institutions need the liquidity that new highs provide in order to exit a big position.

Using a weekly RSI above 80 is a good rule of thumb, but it is not perfect. There are stocks that remain overbought for a very long time and go up 100%–200% after hitting that level. It is rare, but it happens. In 2013, Tesla Motors went from $55 to $200 while its weekly RSI stayed above 80. The hottest stocks of each year often don't care about overbought conditions.

Under overbought conditions, you need to look at everything in context. Those conditions could resolve through time consolidation or through a price pullback.

- Is it a fresh breakout from a humongous base? Have earnings just accelerated? In this case, an overbought condition is likely to be the beginning of a powerful new trend, not the end.
- Is the stock already up more than 800% in the past three years? Do most analysts have a buy rating on the stock? Is the institutional ownership above 90%? Are the CEO and the company featured on the first page of magazines, newspapers, websites? In this case, a severely overbought condition is a good reason for partial profit-taking.

4. When A Trend Is Over

This is usually obvious only in hindsight. There is no perfect exit strategy, but having one is better than nothing. You have to accept that you are not going to catch the entire move. That's OK. You don't have to. The following is a good rule of thumb. Exit when there is:

- A lower low – closes below the most recent time consolidation
- A new 50-day low
- The price closes below 100dma
- The price closes below the 50-week moving average

5. When Your Stop Loss Is Hit

Stops should be placed at a level, which invalidates our investing or trading thesis. This usually means a close below the most recent sideways consolidation.

If Shakespeare were alive today, he would probably be a really good investor:

"I always feel happy. Do you know why? Because I don't expect anything from anyone. Expectations always hurt."

Put "my stocks" in the place of "anyone" and you get good market wisdom to live by.

"I always feel happy. Do you know why? Because I don't expect anything from my stocks. Expectations always hurt."

I sure would like new entries to be profitable, but we have to accept the fact that I am not going to be right every time. If I am not right every time, then it is important to limit my losses to a minimum.

There are times when everything will look perfect and you will pull the trigger and still be wrong. Don't worry about it. It happens. Being wrong is not a choice. Staying wrong is.

I try to stay longer with the stocks that make me happy—the stocks that make me money. I try to kick the stocks that make me sad—the ones that make me lose money. I don't expect to catch big winners every time. I definitely expect to be wrong on some occasions, but I always know how much I have at risk, and so should you. Never let one investment decide your destiny.

Most people simple cannot believe that a market leader could decline 50% or even more than 80% from its high, despite the fact that financial history is full of examples of old leaders having substantial pullbacks.

If you spend enough time investing, eventually you will realize that the three smartest words in the field are "Never say never." All big winners, without an exception, experience a deep pullback at one point of their price cycle. We are talking about a decline of 40%, 50% or more. Some of those stocks recover and offer good secondary buy opportunities. But many never recover. These are the ones from which we have to protect our portfolio and confidence.

The opportunity cost of sticking to your losers is not being able to redeploy that cash to new winners. Sure, they might end up recovering, but in the meantime there will probably be stocks that will do a lot better.

The market is an opportunity machine, and it will deliver a lot of fat pitches in your trading career. You just have to make sure that you are in a position to take advantage of them. You do that by cutting your losses, limiting your drawdown, and protecting your capital and confidence.

About Diversification And Position Sizing

They say that diversification is the only free lunch. They also say that diversification protects wealth, and concentration could help to create it. What is your approach to diversification? Do you like to bet big and put all your eggs in one basket, or do you prefer to play it safe and spread the risk?

Entrepreneurs put all their money, time, and social capital (reputation) in one place. Not all succeed, but those who do enjoy huge payback. Those who don't make it the first time just find a job to pay the bills before pursuing another idea.

Venture capitalists (people who invest in entrepreneurs and their ideas) are much more conservative. On the surface, venture capitalists might look like riverboat gamblers who invest in startups without defined product or revenue, run by fearless kids with zero experience. In reality, they never put all their money in one idea for one simple reason: there are no sure things.

Entrepreneurs and venture capitalists have direct influence on the success of their efforts. There is no guarantee, but they are more or less in control of their own destiny. Public investors, on the other side, have very little control over how a company operates or how the rest of the market will decide to price it. You could speculate, based on experience and forward-looking thinking, where a stock is likely to go, but you could never be 100% sure that it will happen. No one knows the future, which means that some form of diversification makes sense for you.

One great stock idea could change your life if you hold it long enough to make a difference, but you should always have more than one good stock idea, because one could go wrong for various unforeseeable reasons. Don't let one stock wreck the wonders of the stock market for you. It is totally normal and acceptable to be wrong. You just have to make sure that you live to invest another day.

The most important market rule is to always hold yourself responsible for your investments. It is fine to borrow other people's ideas. You don't have to be first in order to make money in the stock market, but you should never transfer responsibility and point fingers. You can't blame anyone—not insiders, not the CEO, not dark pools and institutions.

You need several ideas, but how many exactly?

One of the most successful investors of all time, Warren Buffett, advises most non-professionals to own well-diversified, low-fee indexes like SPY or QQQ. He advises professional investors to limit their holdings to six names, so they can get to know them better. I personally believe that there is a middle ground that would better fit the lifestyle and goals of most of us. Owning 10–12 stocks by allocating 5–10% of your capital to each is a good alternative.

When you allocate 10% of your capital to one idea and your stop loss is 10% below your entry, the most you could lose would be 1% of your capital. I can live with that. If that idea doubles, then the contribution to your total capital would be 10%.

Chapter 9
The Stock Market Is An Opportunity Machine

"The stock market is not the kind of game in which one party loses what another wins. It is the kind of game in which, over certain periods of time, nearly everyone may win, or nearly everyone may lose." – James Grant

Nothing is Guaranteed to Anyone

Warren Buffett is a huge fan of Coca Cola, not only as an investor, but also as a consumer. Here is a story he told at the University of Florida in 1998:

"Coke Cola IPO-ed in 1919 for $40. A year later, it was $19. You can always find a few reasons why that was not a good time to buy it, but if you bought 1 share at $40 and re-invested the dividends, you would have $5 million today. This factor overrides everything—all macro concerns you could have. There is never a perfect time to buy a great business; there is always a reason to worry, but you should also know when it is wise to worry at all. For things that are unimportant or unknown, you should not worry. If you are right about the business, you will make a lot of money over time."

Buffett also added that if he had to put all his money in one stock for the next 20 years, he definitely would not mind if it were Coca Cola. Well, for the 17 years after his speech, the nominal return of Coca Cola was 23%. Not 23% per year, but 23% for the entire period. The S & P 500 returned 85% for the same time (ex-dividends).

Proper market timing matters, regardless of the virtues of the underlying company. Just because a business has strong brands and pricing power, it doesn't necessarily make it a great investment. There are no sure things in the market. Nothing is guaranteed to anyone.

Warren Buffett jokes that he prefers simple businesses that could be run by idiots, because sooner or later they will be. He hates uncertainty and wants to invest in companies that are likely to earn a lot more 10 years from now. He loves strong brands, because they have high mind share and pricing power.

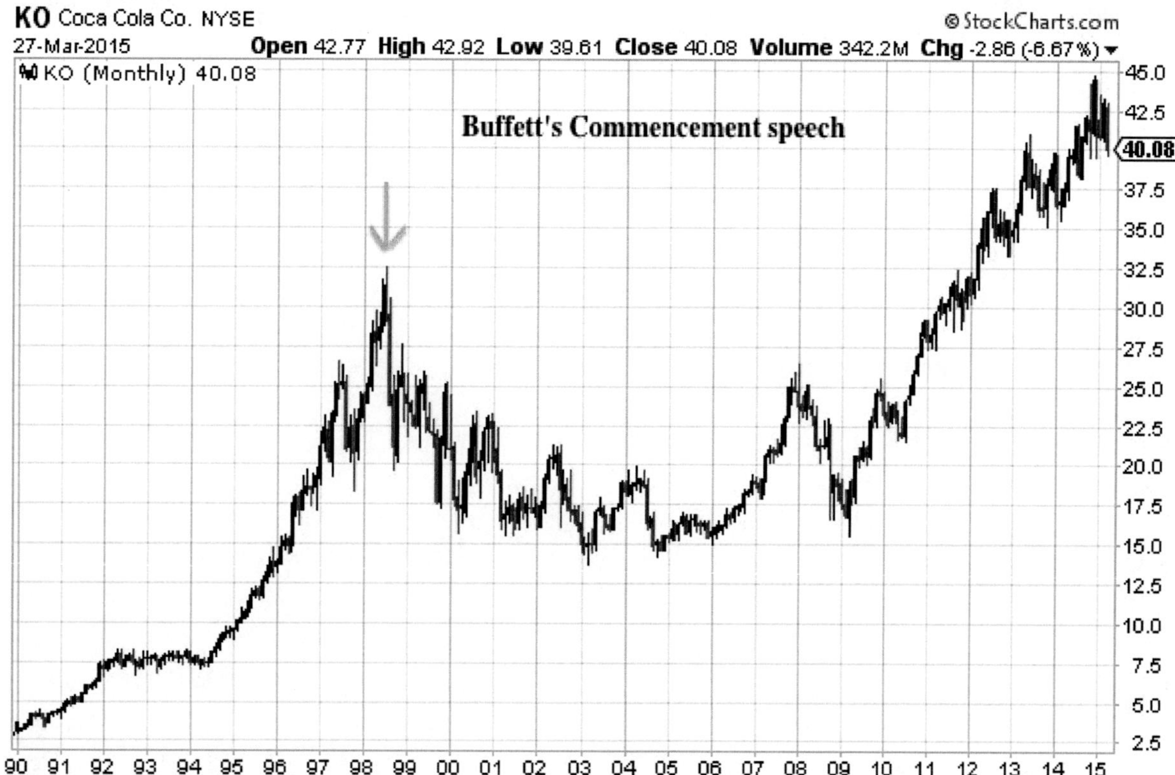

Mr. Buffett advises that if you are long-term investor, you should not choose your stocks based on the impact their industry will have on society but based on how durable their competitive advantage is. The truth is that very few companies could sustain their competitive advantage for a very long time. And if they do, the market often prices that in their stocks today, so their future return is hardly a big surprise. Companies that are well-known and easily predictable tend to deliver average market returns, at best—as was the case with Coca Cola in the past 17 years.

There Are Different Types Of Trends

In markets and in life, there are trends that last only a year, and there are trends that last several decades. You could make a lot of money in both types of trends if you learn how to properly time your exits and entries.

Financial history is full of examples of stocks that went up 300%, 500%, or 1000% in a few quarters and then gave most of it back for various reasons. Earnings growth naturally slowed down, competition erased margins, investors' expectations about the future of the stocks declined significantly, the general market went into correction, etc.

Blackberry went from $2 to $150 in five years, and then it dropped 95% in the following four years. Just because we don't know if a company can sustain its competitive advantage for more than a few years or remain a market leader, should we just miss on a several hundred or even several thousand percent return?

From 2003 to 2008, U.S. Steel Corp. went from $10 to $180. Over the next year, it gave back almost everything and it went back to $20. In early 2015, U.S. Steel is trading below its IPO price from 1991, providing 24 years of nothing for those that just bought and held on (hoped).

You don't need to a ride a trend for 10 years in order to make a difference in your returns. There are plenty of decent trends that last only a year or two and deliver substantial profits for those who have an exit strategy.

Timing Matters

Netflix has been one of the craziest stocks in the past decade. There were four distinct stages:

- From 2009 to mid-2011, it went from $30 to $300.
- It tanked to $60 in four short months, constituting an 80% drop in a little over a quarter.
- It spent about a year of going nowhere, frustrating both bulls and bears, eventually reaching the ultimate level of neglect and indifference. It was even kicked out from the Nasdaq 100 near the end of 2012, when it was a 90-dollar stock.
- In January 2013, it emerged to new 52-week highs and went up to $500 per share.

How is it possible for a stock to fluctuate so much inside four years? Would you call this efficient? Netflix is the poster child for inefficient markets. The company can't be valued properly as it grows, shrinks, and grows, so you have surprises. How can you say that timing doesn't matter for such a stock—or, for that matter, for any stock?

The only constants in financial markets are change and uncertainty. Not only business environments change, but also people's perceptions of stocks change. Keurig Green Mountain Coffee (GMCR) went from making a new all-time high at $10 in March 2009 to $115 in September 2011. Then it pulled back. By the summer of 2012, it was trading under $20. In early 2015, it is back above 125.

Trends come and go. Some last only a few quarters. Others last several years. We don't know how long a trend is going to last and we don't need to in order to benefit from it. Proper equity selection is of utmost importance. The most important part of equity selection is timing.

X USX-US Steel Group, Inc. NYSE
©StockCharts.com
27-Mar-2015
Open 23.92 High 25.62 Low 21.28 Close 24.78 Volume 175.4M Chg +0.83 (+3.47%)
X (Monthly) 24.78
24.78
1999 2000 2001 2002 2003 2004 2005 2006 2007 2008 2009 2010 2011 2012 2013 2014 2015

GMCR Keurig Green Mountain, Inc. Nasdaq GS
©StockCharts.com
27-Mar-2015
Open 127.58 High 130.76 Low 112.80 Close 113.20 Volume 31.4M Chg -14.06 (-11.05%)
GMCR (Monthly) 113.20
113.20
1999 2000 2001 2002 2003 2004 2005 2006 2007 2008 2009 2010 2011 2012 2013 2014 2015

Is Timing Equally Important If You Invest In Well-diversified Indexes?

Some argue that timing is irrelevant when it comes to dollar-cost averaging in low-fee indexes. Tell that to Japanese investors. Between 1970 and 1981, Japanese stocks returned on average 21% annually. To put things in perspective, $10,000 invested in the Nikkei in 1970 was worth $450,000 by 1989. Then everything turned upside down, and in the next 25 years, Nikkei's average annual performance dropped to -2%. Again, to put things in perspective, $10,000 invested in Nikkei in 1990 was worth about $6,000 by the end of 2014. Suddenly dollar-cost averaging in a single index doesn't seem like a sure bet, does it?

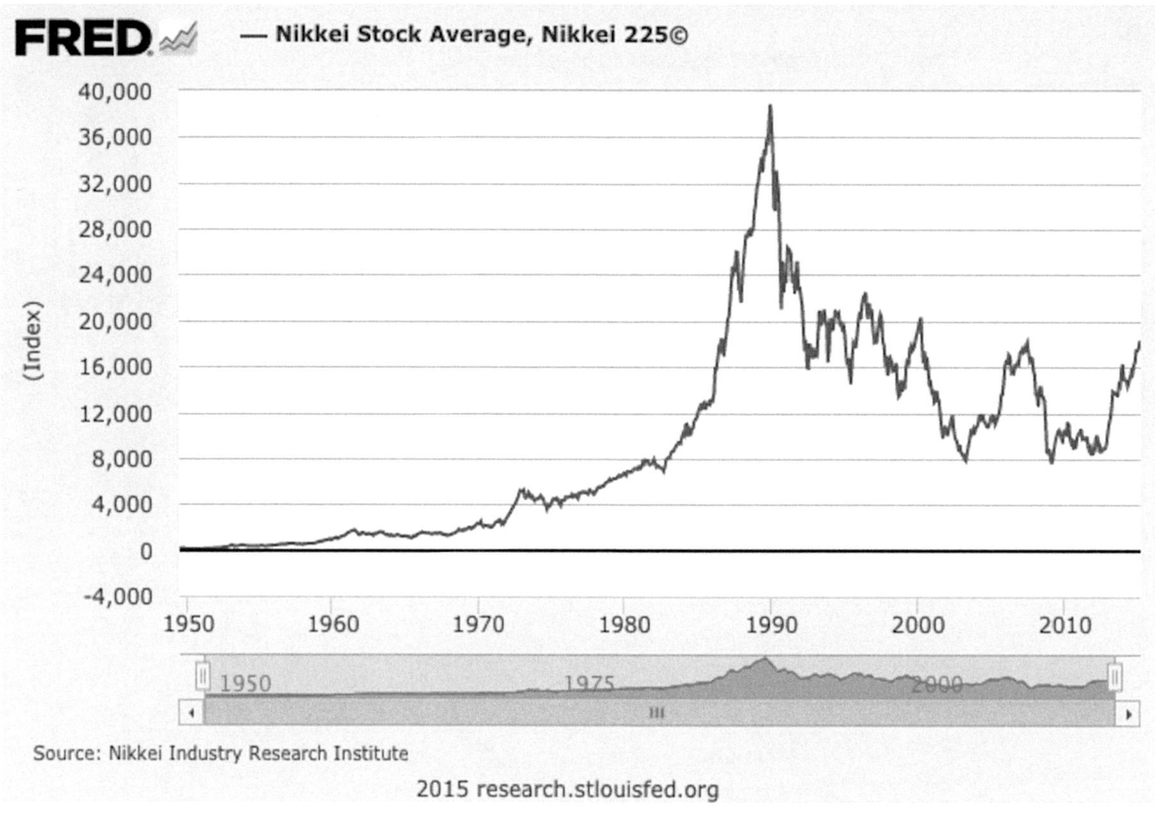

You don't need to study Japan to understand the cyclicality in overall market returns. What happened in Japan has happened in almost every capital market.

They say a picture is worth a thousand words. Look at the following two graphs, showing the S & P 500 (or its equivalent at the time) return since 1903. Strong periods lasted 10–15 years on average, and then they were followed by periods of disappointing results.

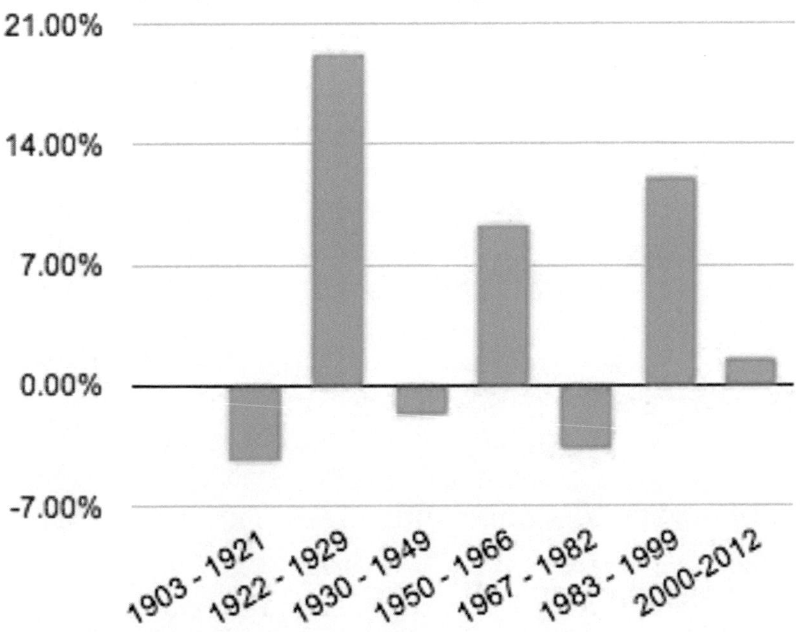
S & P 500 Average Annual Return
(Capital Gains Only)
21.00%
14.00%
7.00%
0.00%
-7.00%
1903 - 1921
1922 - 1929
1930 - 1949
1950 - 1966
1967 - 1982
1983 - 1999
2000-2012

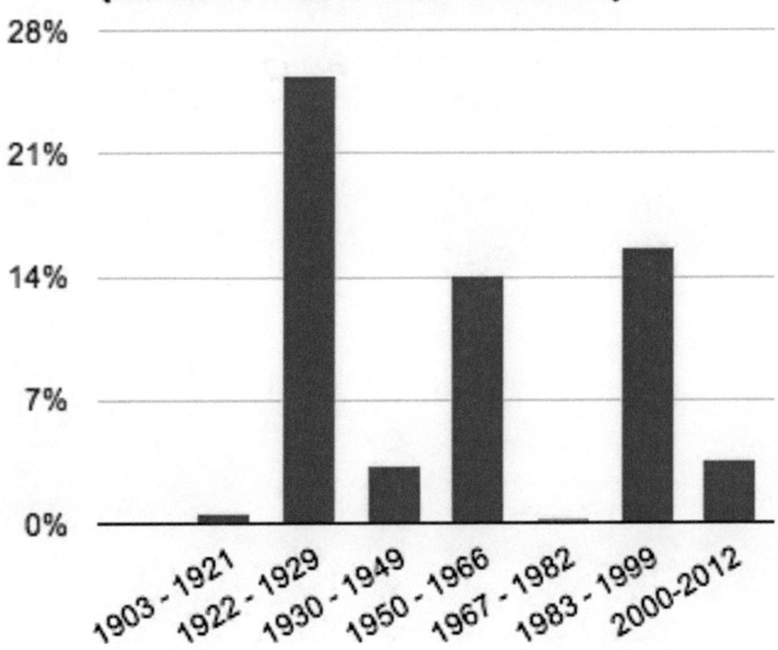
S & P 500 Average Annual Return
(With Dividends Reinvested)
28%
21%
14%
7%
0%
1903 - 1921
1922 - 1929
1930 - 1949
1950 - 1966
1967 - 1982
1983 - 1999
2000-2012

The S& P 500 finally managed to clear new all-time highs in 2013, when It gained 32% for the year (including dividends). In 2014, the large cap U.S. index appreciated another 13.5%.

The big question is, what's next?

Why the Next 10 Years Will Be A Stock-Pickers' Market

In late 1999, Warren Buffet told the world that the next 17 years will be a lot more challenging for the stock market than the previous 17 years that delivered record gains. Buffett added that he would be really surprised if the stock market achieved a return higher than nominal GDP growth.

There were only four ways to achieve higher returns:

1) If interest rates dropped significantly. They did—from 6% to under 3%.
2) If corporate earnings increased their cut in GDP. They did—from 6% to almost 11%.
3) If valuation went even higher than it was. It was already too stretched, so it was normal to see some form of mean-reversion there.
4) If you are a great stock picker.

Buffett's educated guess turned out to be spot on. By 2009, the S & P 500 dropped 30%. Between 1999 and 2014, the S & P 500 nominal return (ex-dividends) was 43%. Nominal GDP growth was 58% for the same period.

16
15
14
13
12
11
10
9
8
7
6
5
4
3
2
1
0
Black Tuesday
Black Monday
2.24%
1880
1890
1900
1910
1920
1930
1940
1950
1960
1970
1980
1990
2000
2010

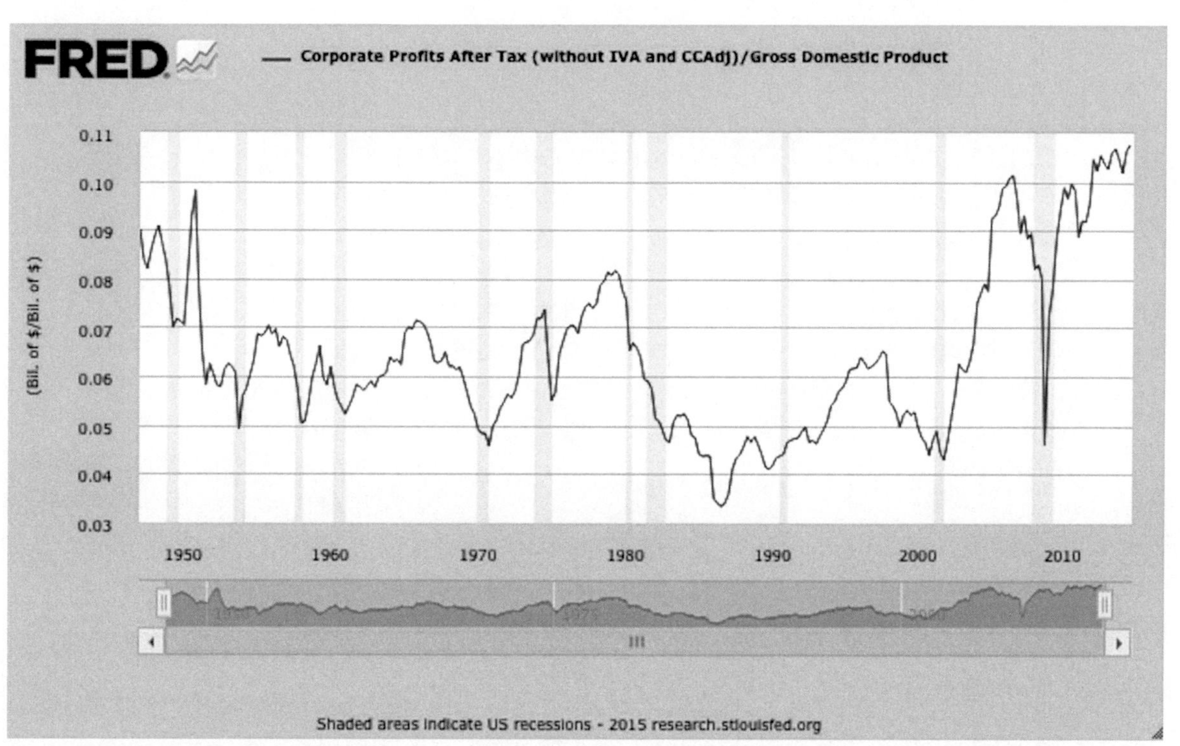
FRED
Corporate Profits After Tax (without IVA and CCAdj)/Gross Domestic Product
(Bil. of $/Bil. of $)
0.11
0.10
0.09
0.08
0.07
0.06
0.05
0.04
0.03
1950
1960
1970
1980
1990
2000
2010
Shaded areas indicate US recessions - 2015 research.stlouisfed.org

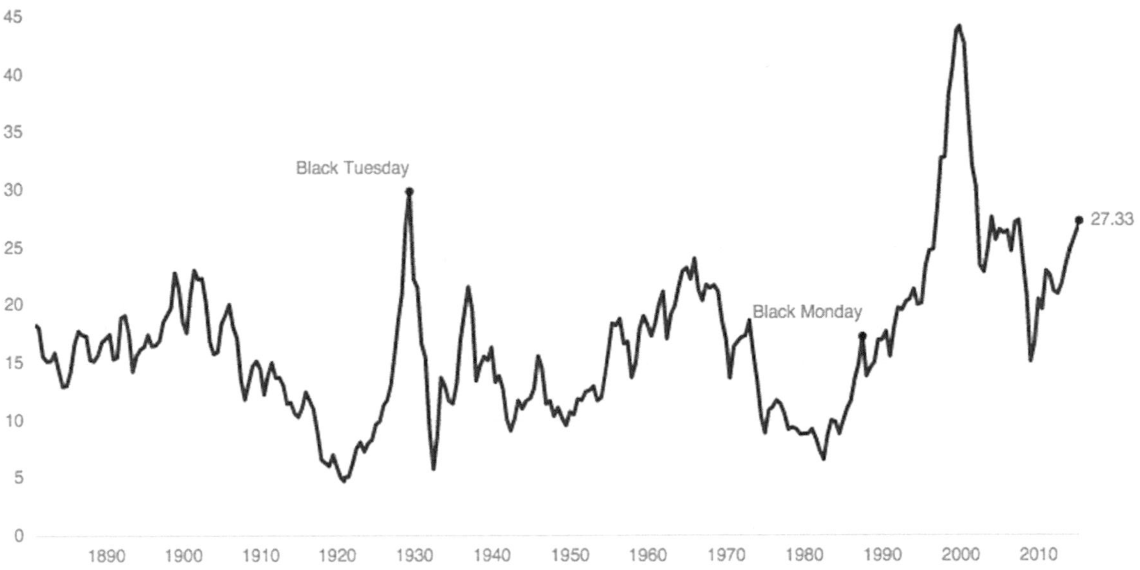

Let's take a look at the current standing of the three major factors that could drive long-term profits for the stock market in general:

1) Interest rates are at record lows under 3%. Unless the U.S. becomes the next Japan (which would mean extremely low GDP growth), interest rates are not likely to go much lower, and therefore they are not going to be of much help to stocks.
2) Corporate profits as a percentage of GDP are at record highs near 11%. Financial history and logic say that their cut of GDP is not likely to increase much from those levels;
3) Sentiment/Valuation – valuations are a little stretched, but nowhere near 2000's levels. Stocks could get a boost here, but I would not bet on it.

Assuming that the three factors above won't have a negative impact on stocks (they could easily do so), the total market performance in the next 10 years will depend only on two factors:

A) Nominal GDP growth. If we assume about 4% nominal growth and 2% dividends, the best-case scenario is about 6% average annual return, which is not too bad, actually.
B) Your stock picking skills – anything above or below that 6% annually will depend on your ability to pick stocks and allocate to different assets.

The numbers suggest that we are likely headed for another challenging decade for stock market investors. This is a challenge that is also an opportunity.

The period between 2000 and 2010 brought a lot of turbulence. We had two "once in 100 years" storms: the big correction in early 2000, when the Nasdaq Composite declined 80%, and 2008/2009, when the S&P 500 had a 57% plunge. The very same decade also brought us epic bull markets in commodities and emerging markets, monstrous trends in consumer discretionary, and technology names like Apple, Google, Monster Energy, Chipotle, Blackberry, and Netflix. These are just a few of the huge multi-year moves that happened during the so called "lost decade."

Even if the next 10 years turn out to be just as volatile and crazy as the first decade of this century, and even if the major equity indexes deliver negative returns for the decade and we go through several humongous corrections, there will be plenty of opportunities for shrewd traders and investors to consistently grow wealth. Some things never change in the market. One of these things is the existence of great growth and recovery stories.

The biggest market secret is not that given enough time, everything is cyclical. It is not that Buy and Hold Forever works or doesn't work depending on the different market environment. It is not that the common wisdom of one investment era is a terrible advice for another investment era. It is not that every big market supercycle lasts long enough for investors to forget what it felt like investing in the previous cycle. It is not that every bubble has led to a deep correction, and every bust has put the foundations for another major uptrend. It is not that the winners of each new bull market were always different than the ones from the previous bull market. The biggest market secret is that the stock market has always been a market of stocks with huge divergence in the performance of individual equities. No matter how the market averages perform over any 10-year period, there will always be individual stocks that will crush the averages.

The market is an opportunity machine. Over the next century, there will be some incredible new and old trends that will deliver amazing opportunities for the savvy investors. We will mine asteroids, have robots do most of our work, interact with intelligent machines in various new ways, travel to space, and build cities on Mars. Biotech will change the way we do everything, and it will enhance our life exponentially. All those trends will create hundreds of stocks that will go up 1000% or a lot more, and these profits will be there for the taking by anyone who knows how. The beauty of the market is that we don't need to know which technologies are going to change the world and which companies are going to benefit the most. The market will tell you which stocks to buy and when to buy them. All you need to do is to listen. This book is a great guide for how to do it.

You should always think for yourself and take every opinion with a grain of salt. In this case, it is obvious that we are biased. Our financial research business and our personal market approaches are based on the deeply ingrained belief that markets are inefficient and could be beaten with proper equity selection and risk management. We are not telling you to stop dollar-cost averaging in low-fee indexes and learn how to pick stocks. We are just sharing what has worked for us and where we will continue to focus our efforts.

About the Authors

Ivaylo Ivanov (@ivanhoff) is a full-time trader. He has been trading equities and options for almost ten years.

Ivaylo is Co-founder of socialleverage50.com, where he runs a stock-picking and risk management premium service.

Mr. Ivanov is the author of The Next Apple – How To Find Stocks That Could Go Up 1000%, The 5 Secrets To Highly Profitable Swing Trading and the editor of The StockTwits Edge - 40 Setups from Real Market Pros.

Ivaylo's work is regularly featured on Bloomberg, WSJ, Yahoo Finance, Reuters, CNN Money, UT San Diego, Traders Magazine, Abnormal Returns, Real Clear Markets, The Reformed Broker.

Follow me on Twitter and StockTwits: @ivanhoff @SL50
ivanhoff.com socialleverage50.com sl-50.tumblr.com

Howard Lindzon has more than 20 years experience in the financial community acting in both an entrepreneurial and investing capacity. With a unique vision for starting, managing, and successfully advising innovative companies, Lindzon is the public-face of the Social Leverage entities.

In 2008 Lindzon co-founded StockTwits, recently named "one of the top 10 most innovative companies in web" by FastCompany and one of the "50 best websites" by Time (where he invented the "cashtag").

Previously, Lindzon created more than 400 original videos on Wallstrip, acquired by $CBS in 2007. Lindzon stepped down from his operational role as CEO of StockTwits on December 31, 2013, to focus on the next phase of Social Leverage. As acting Chairman, Lindzon's connection to StockTwits along with his hedge fund experience, give Social Leverage access to a community of professionals who can evaluate fintech opportunities.

Follow me on Twitter and StockTwits: @howardlindzon
howardlindzon.com

Disclaimer

The views expressed in this book are the personal views of the author only and do not necessarily reflect the views of the author's employer. The views expressed reflect the current views of author as of the date hereof and the author does not undertake to advise you of any changes in the views expressed herein. In addition, the views expressed do not necessarily reflect the opinions of any investment professional at the author's employer, and may not be reflected in the strategies and products that his employer offers. The author's employer may have positions (long or short) or engage in securities transactions that are not consistent with the information and views expressed in this presentation. The author assumes no duty to, nor undertakes to update forward looking statements. No representation or warranty, express or implied, is made or given by or on behalf of the author, the author's employer or any other person as to the accuracy and completeness or fairness of the information contained in this presentation and no responsibility or liability is accepted for any such information. By accepting this book, the recipient acknowledges its understanding.

.

Made in the USA
San Bernardino, CA
08 July 2017